Written on
Your Heart

Bob Arsenault

WESTBOW
P R E S S®
A DIVISION OF THOMAS NELSON
& ZONDERVAN

This book is a work of non-fiction. Unless otherwise noted, the author and the publisher make no explicit guarantees as to the accuracy of the information contained in this book and in some cases, names of people and places have been altered to protect their privacy.

WestBow Press books may be ordered through booksellers or by contacting:

WestBow Press
A Division of Thomas Nelson & Zondervan
1663 Liberty Drive
Bloomington, IN 47403
www.westbowpress.com
1 (866) 928-1240

Because of the dynamic nature of the Internet, any web addresses or links contained in this book may have changed since publication and may no longer be valid. The views expressed in this work are solely those of the author and do not necessarily reflect the views of the publisher, and the publisher hereby disclaims any responsibility for them.

Any people depicted in stock imagery provided by Thinkstock are models, and such images are being used for illustrative purposes only. Certain stock imagery © Thinkstock.

ISBN: 978-1-5127-9373-4 (sc)
ISBN: 978-1-5127-9374-1 (hc)
ISBN: 978-1-5127-9372-7 (e)

Library of Congress Control Number: 2017910923

Print information available on the last page.

WestBow Press rev. date: 12/21/2017

Table of Contents

Dedication

I wouldn't be the man I am today without the unfailing love of my wife.

My children brighten my world with their love, laughter, and affection. Ethan, your creativity is inspiring. Elliot, your teachable heart is honorable. Brinkley, your joy is infectious. This book is my legacy I leave for you. Seek God and you will find him; that is his promise.

I wouldn't be on this journey called a walk with God if not for my older brother, Mike. Thanks for having the heart of Andrew, who wanted his brother Peter to meet this amazing man Jesus.

My dear friend Kevin McDaniel, thanks for setting the bar high and challenging me to begin this quest of memorizing books of the Bible over twenty-five years ago.

Foreword

I've told you these things for a purpose: that
my joy might be your joy, and your joy wholly
mature. This is my command: Love one another
the way I loved you. This is the very best way to
love. Put your life on the line for your friends.
You are my friends when you do the things I
command you. I'm no longer calling you servants
because servants don't understand what their
master is thinking and planning. No, I've named
you friends because I've let you in on everything
I've heard from the Father. (John 15:11–15 THE
MESSAGE)

It strikes me that when Jesus came into this world with the all-
encompassing global mission to save it, he did not come seeking
leaders, the talented, the sharp, the rich, the influential, or the
high powered. These attributes were not on his radar. He came
looking for friends.

I'm nearing sixty years old. I've been the young whippersnapper
and the wise old veteran. I've been a talented prized possession
and too expensive to keep. I've been up and I've been down. I've
been on top and I've been on the bottom . . . and every place
between. I'm also still young enough to visit all those places again.
Here's what I've learned along the way: If you have found a good

friend in life, you've done well. If you have found more than one good friend, you've done very well.

I hope you do not think these are the musings of someone jaded by all that life dishes out. Life has definitely done some "dishing," but I've certainly not been exempt from doing the same. What this simpleton has gleaned over sixty years of climbing ladders, chasing dollars, trying to impress, getting ahead, surviving, and constantly self-reinventing himself can be summed up this way: the importance of friendship. I am honored to be counted as a friend, and I am also humbled and grateful to have some to call my own. To all my friends, it has been my great pleasure to know you and to be known by you.

Circa 1989 I met a friend, your author, whom I have always called Bobby. From day one until now, he has been a devoted, loyal friend to God and also to me. I met Bobby years ago when I was working in the Boston Campus Ministry, which also included Bridgewater State University. He was one of the students in the BSU ministry. He was and is a leader. He had a pure and innocent faith that was growing because he was seeking, knocking, and learning. We tirelessly worked the ministry together. We played Ping-Pong, lifted weights, and threw the football around. We had lots of fun. We also honestly shared our thoughts and dreams with each other. Over the course of time, our friendship deepened.

Several years after Bobby and I met, my wife and I were asked to lead a ministry in Springfield, Massachusetts. We were encouraged to invite some close friends to join us. I asked Bobby to come with us. Why? He helped me be a better version of me. His faith boosted my confidence, and I believed that if someone like Bobby came with us—someone so dedicated, reliable, and trustworthy—our ministry would be a success. It was comforting to know that someone working with me cared as much about the work as I did. Plus, it was just good to always have a friend nearby. I could give you a hundred reasons why it made sense to invite Bobby to come with us. But simply put, he was and is my friend. I loved being around him. I wanted him with us, and I am so glad he came.

These were amazing times. Our ministry was challenging but also fun, and our church was growing. I may have put it differently many years ago, but today I would simply say that we were just making friends. We played Wiffle ball and ultimate Frisbee, and we hiked local trails. We played, laughed, hung out, and constantly had people over for dinner. My wife and I must have fed thirty to fifty college students each week, including Bobby. It was a blast. Memories of friendship that will last a lifetime. In the midst of all the fun, we were also seeking God, growing in our understanding of him, building our ministry, and doing all this with friends. Lives were impacting other lives.

I once shared with Bobby that I had memorized whole books of the Bible and how I hoped this practice would help guide my thoughts and aspirations in life. It did. With this in mind, I started a training class for young, aspiring ministry leaders in Springfield. Those who took the class were required to memorize 2 Timothy. This letter was written by a seasoned apostle to a young minister, encouraging him with sage words such as, "And the things you have heard me say in the presence of many witnesses entrust to reliable men who will also be qualified to teach others" (2 Timothy 2:2). Given the passion we had to turn the world upside down, it seemed appropriate for us to write this book on our hearts.

Memorizing scared everyone at first, but the class of twenty-plus successfully memorized this book. Although Bobby "kicked and screamed the whole time," he memorized it too. Accomplishing this goal inspired him to go above and beyond memorizing 2 Timothy. Over the last twenty-five years, he has continued his quest to memorize other books of the Bible. He's also enjoyed a successful life and career over the years. He has a wonderful wife, Lori, and a sweet, sweet family he dearly loves. As a side note, Bobby married way out of his league. I'm proud of the man he has become.

One of my favorite memories of our friendship happened at a pool in Durham, North Carolina, many years ago. Bobby and I had long since parted company, but we occasionally kept up with a phone call. At this point we hadn't talked for months. One afternoon, I was sitting at our neighborhood pool with my family and some friends. I watched this guy walk into the pool area and I thought, "That guy looks just like Bobby Arsenault." Unexpectedly and from out of nowhere, Bobby walked toward me flashing his big grin. Clearly laughing at me, as he saw my shock and surprise.

One of the great things about good friends is that they always show up. They show up in our thoughts, our dreams, and our good feelings as we think about the past, live in the present, and plan for the future. They show up when we need them, and sometimes they even show up when we think we don't need them. But they show up! And once in a blue moon, they show up at the pool. I don't think I have ever felt more respected, needed, loved, and wanted than I did in that moment. I love my friend Bobby Arsenault.

We continue to share a vision to change the world for Jesus. However, in our younger years, we were determined to do it in a hurry. Although this desire is a noble one, I've learned in the course of sixty years that the world changes only at the speed of friendship. Jesus knew this. I'm thankful for his friendship, and for the other friends I've made over the years. It is my prayer that *Written on Your Heart* will motivate you to write Scripture on your heart so you can build a better friendship with Jesus and his disciples as we impact this lost world.

Kevin R. McDaniel CPC, CLP
WindRiver Strategies
Executive Coach / Keynote Speaker / Leadership Trainer
Member: International Coach Federation / International Association of Coaching
Emergenetics Certified
Email: kevin@windriverstrategies.net
www.windriverstrategies.net

Introduction

Life-changing moments. How can one explain them? All of us have turning points in our lives, those moments when we say, "Wow, can you imagine if I had made a different decision all those years ago, instead of the one I did?" Who can understand the mystery of choices? When I see God, I look forward to asking him, "Lord, what if I had decided to move to Atlanta in 1992 instead of going to Springfield, Massachusetts? What would my life have been like? What impact would that journey have had on my life and the lives of others? Would I still be faithful to you? Who would be my friends? Would I have memorized books of the bible?" The quality of our lives comes down to the decisions we make *and act upon every day.*

This book is a story about how one decision I made early in my Christian life forever changed the course of my walk with God. It paved a foundation that has sustained my faith through the many difficulties I've faced over the years.

I became a Christian in June 1987. I graduated college in 1991. Having been accepted into Emory University's theology program, I was excited to embark on a new journey in the area of academics. But just six weeks before leaving for Atlanta from Boston, God stepped in and challenged me to reconsider my plans: "Many are the plans in a man's heart, but it is the Lord's purpose that prevails" (Proverbs 19:21). I received a call from Kevin McDaniel, a dear friend who was the campus minister at the University of Massachusetts in Boston. After some quick pleasantries, he got to the point.

"Bob, I have some good news. Debbie and I were asked to lead a team of people to Springfield, Massachusetts. Our mission is to help grow and build a church in that city."

"That's great, Kevin," I said. "I wish you the best in your endeavor. I'm heading to Atlanta in a few weeks."

He asked me what my plans were.

"I want to become a minister."

He then asked, "Would you be willing to forgo your plans to get a master's degree to come with us to Springfield? We want to build a great beacon of light for the people of Western Mass."

My heart began beating quickly. I didn't want to give up my dream of getting a degree in theology, but I knew Kevin's call was no accident; it was God's way of compelling me to serve the church in a greater way. I told him I'd have to pray about it.

For the next few days, a wrestling match ensued between God and me. I weighed the pros and cons of going to Springfield as well as continuing my plan to attend Emory. I prayed often. I made lists. I sought guidance from brothers in the Lord about what to do. I prayed some more.

After a few days, I called Kevin. "I'm in. I look forward to heading to Springfield with you and the others."

I didn't know it at the time, but my role eventually would be to assist Kevin as a campus minister at the University of Massachusetts in Amherst. My time in Springfield was some of the best and most challenging years of my life. It was there I began the journey of memorizing books of the Bible.

It was a brisk spring day in 1992 when a small group of us young men and women were invited to attend a ministry training class Kevin was teaching. Our purpose was to learn how to be more effective leaders for God and his church. The class was to last several weeks.

Kevin laid out the expectations for the ministry training class.

One was to memorize the book of 2 Timothy. All of us looked at each other in disbelief. I knew what Philip must have felt when Jesus asked him where they should find bread for thousands of people. I envision Philip's incredulity as he scratched his head and said, "Eight months wages would not buy enough bread for each one to have a bite" (John 6:7).

I thought Kevin had lost his mind. Never mind memorizing a whole book of the Bible—I could barely remember someone's name immediately after we were introduced. I frequently forget where I put my car keys. *He wants me to memorize what? Doesn't he know I barely graduated high school?* If it hadn't been for a friend helping me with my SATs, I probably wouldn't have attended college. As a matter of fact, during my first semester as a college freshman at the University of Massachusetts in Amherst, I scored a whopping 1.0 GPA. I grew up with parents who were deaf and had minimal academic expectations of me. As a result, I had low expectations for myself.

I was not blessed with a gifted memory, and I was not a scholar—far from it. I was an average student at best. Quite frankly, it was only by the grace of God that I completed high school.

Faced with this current expectation of memorizing a whole book of the Bible, I recalled a special experience I'd had as a young Christian. When I was about two months old in the faith, I attended a conference in Boston. I went to a class taught by a preacher named Andy Fleming. I don't recall much about what he said because it was over thirty years ago. But, one story he shared has stuck with me over the span of time.

When he was a missionary in Papua New Guinea, many tribal men and woman became Christians. They were excited to learn about God's Word in their native language. In fact, many of them memorized long passages of Scripture—even entire books of the Bible.

I walked out of that class with my brother and asked, "Did he really say those Christians in the tribe memorized books of the Bible, like Romans and Hebrews?"

"Yes, he did!" he responded.

I was amazed! I thought memorizing large chunks of Scripture was impossible. How could these people, with no so-called formal education, memorize whole books of the Bible?

Over the years, I've cherished this incredible story. Perhaps something in me said, "If they can do it, so can I." Many years have passed since the conference, and I thought maybe I was imagining or embellishing the details, so I recently contacted Andy to be sure I had my facts correct.

He quickly confirmed. "You heard me correctly. When I was a missionary in Papua New Guinea, some of the Christians memorized long pieces of Scripture and whole books."

I was thankful for his confirmation. Little did I know, what I thought was impossible would be possible. It's amazing to think that God can do more than all we ask or imagine.

I wanted to ask Kevin, "Can't we memorize Second or Third John instead? One chapter and a few verses?" Something more in line with my ability to memorize. Plus, who enjoys the tedious work of memorizing? It's one thing to remember a song or a short poem, but a book of the Bible with four chapters?

But Kevin was steadfast. If I wanted to pass the class, I had to recite all of 2 Timothy, verbatim.

As a campus minister I couldn't opt out of the class, while my classmates had a choice whether or not to attend. Kevin explained the memorization strategy, why to memorize, and what it required to get it done—hard work, repetition, and more repetition. He made it seem pretty simple. All of us tried to swallow our fear, wondering how we could succeed. Still, we made the commitment to do it and applied whole hearted effort!

At the end of the training program, most of us memorized the entire book. I don't know if any of my fellow students from that class still know 2 Timothy, but I'll never let go of those precious words. It includes some of the most prized verses etched on my heart. Memorizing this book proved I could do more than I thought possible.

The primary goal of *Written on Your Heart* is to share how memorization has affected my life and my walk with God, with the hope that it will inspire you in the same way. I offer suggestions about how to memorize. Truthfully, memorizing Scripture is not easy. It requires a lot of repetition. After twenty-three years, I still regularly recite the passages I've memorized.

Aside from it helping me grow closer to God, it's also a good way to exercise my brain. As Linda Melone in *Everyday Health* wrote:

> Just as lifting weights adds lean muscle to your body and helps you retain more muscle in your later years, researchers now believe that following a brain-healthy lifestyle and performing regular targeted brain exercises can also increase your brain's cognitive reserve.[1]

Another article in *How to Improve Your Brain* says, "A strong memory depends on the health and vitality of your brain."[2] How can we keep our brains healthy and vital? By using it, by doing mental exercises. Memorizing God's Word is one way to exercise and develop brain strength. It's also food for the heart and soul.

Turning points are life changing. They can be promises we make to God, ourselves, and our families that we'll stick to a task no matter the challenges. We'll get it done or die trying. No matter how intimidating the task is, we'll keep on keeping on until it's complete.

Memorization has revolutionized my life, and it can transform yours, too. Since that spring day in 1992, I have memorized the gospel of John, Colossians, Philippians, 2 Timothy, Psalm 8, 19, 23, 51, 63, 100, 148, and Hebrews 11. It hasn't been an easy journey, but it's been amazingly rewarding. These books have given me tremendous knowledge into how to live life and, more importantly, how to have a deeper walk with God. The gospel of John has opened up the most awesome insights into the wonderful life of Jesus.

Maybe you're asking, "Why memorize entire books of the Bible? Is that really necessary?" I hope this book will answer these questions and more. You may never have had a desire to memorize whole books, but perhaps I can entice you to memorize more of God's Word than you thought possible. Let's begin the journey.

PART ONE

More Precious Than Gold

Chapter 1
Walk with Treasure

*P*erhaps you already realize that there is something special and unique about the Bible. Allow me to reinforce what you may already know. I recently watched *The Book of Eli*, starring Denzel Washington as the title character. It is a great movie- a must see! He encounters a lot of tough guys in his post-apocalyptic mission to find a place of solace for him and his treasure—the only surviving Bible. He protects this book at all costs. Eli overcomes many obstacles in making sure the enemy doesn't get hold of the book to use for evil means.

Eventually, the enemy captures it and shoots Eli, leaving him for dead. However, thanks to the help of a friend, Eli survives, and together they make the journey to a place of solace—the island of Alcatraz. When Eli approaches the gates on the island, the guards demand, "What business do you have here?"

"I'm here to deliver the Bible," he says.

The person in charge of the library on Alcatraz is solely responsible for saving and archiving books of antiquity. When he asks Eli for the Bible, Eli tells him, "Grab some paper and a pen and write what is shared." Eli starts reciting from memory Genesis 1:1, "In the beginning God created the heavens and the earth." Because Eli has the entire Bible memorized, he continues to dictate the entire sixty-six books.

As the movie draws to a close, you see page after page with words of Scripture on them lying on a table. A man is feverishly writing the words Eli is sharing. Once the librarian finishes, you see the pages compiled into a hardback—the Bible. Then it is placed on a library shelf.

One lesson of the movie is that you can take away the book from someone, but you can't take away the words written on their heart. He or she can share it with anyone and everyone, meditate on it anywhere, and reflect on its meaning any time. Another takeaway is a question I ponder. If I was asked to compile the Bible from memory, how many scriptures could I write on paper?

Gold Rush is a relatively new reality TV show. It's about a few teams of people who go to certain areas of the world to dig for gold. Gold is not easy to find, but whoever finds the most by the end of the season wins. Mining gold requires an immense amount of energy, hours, vehicles, sifting equipment, and much more. The series portrays only the first steps in retrieving the gold from the ground. Many other steps are required to process gold into various products.

What I learned from the series induced me to research more about gold mining, which led me to read *Gold: The Race for the Most Seductive Metal*, a fascinating book revealing what humans will do to mine gold. One part of the book told about the deepest machine-dug hole on the earth, the Mponeng mine, which goes down almost three miles.

> You can stack ten Empire State Buildings on top of one another and that's how deep this hole is. The mine devours as much electricity as a city of 400,000 people. Rivers of water pulse through its plumbing. There are two hundred and thirty-six miles of tunnels that lace through its veins. It is thirty miles longer than the New York City subway system. Every morning 4,000

people vanish into its subterranean web of shafts, ore chutes, and haulage. The temperature in the tunnels reach 140 Fahrenheit and the humidity is 95 percent. Perspiration soaks a person in seconds. It takes 6,000 tons of ice a day to keep the temperature at a bearable eighty-three degrees. Six hundred times a month the mine gets a "seismic event" that shudders through its veins. These men put their lives at risk every day they make the journey down the elevator. And this is just the first phase of getting ore from the earth. The second phase entails building a mill, smashing the ore into powder, feeding it through a complex series of special tanks in which the particles of gold attached themselves to carbon, collect the mess at the end, burn off the dross, and finally pour it into bars.[1]

All that to get gold out of the earth's crust.

Some people will do just about anything to get gold because of its value. Let's look at what David said about the Word of God in Psalm 19:10: "They are more precious than gold, than much pure gold." And Psalm 119:72 says, "The law from your mouth is more precious to me than thousands of pieces of gold and silver."

At the time of this writing, gold is worth about $1,300 an ounce. Ask yourself these questions:

- Would you rather have gold or God's Word?
- Which one is temporary; which is eternal?
- When you die, will you take your gold (money) with you?

Kings and pharaohs have tried to take their earthly riches with them in death by commanding that their treasure be buried with them. But when archeologists discover their tombs, their treasures are still there. Gold, silver, gems, and whatever else the kings valued did not follow them into eternity. We need to be like Moses, who regarded a walk with God of greater value than the treasures of Egypt (Hebrews 11:26). Don't let the Scriptures sit idle on your desk or on your bookshelf! The Bible is the most amazing book in the world. It is filled with spiritual treasure to help you in your quest to be your best for God.

It is astounding to read about what people will do to get gold ore out of the deep recesses of the earth, yet we have a living, breathing, active force from God at our fingertips. But we can often neglect it because we're too busy. We'd rather watch TV than spend time with this treasure.

His Word is more valuable, precious, and beautiful than gold, but we have a hard time consistently reading it, much less memorizing it. I'm frequently amazed at how I have the energy to do strenuous work, exercise for hours, shop, and do things with friends, but when it comes time to read my Bible, that's when I get tired. I just want to sleep! I know you may find that odd or even funny, but it's true. Can you relate? I'm not sure why this happens, but I suspect it has something to do "with our struggle not being against flesh and blood, but against the spiritual forces of evil in the heavenly realms" (Ephesians 6:12). In spite of the challenges and obstacles we face, if we have God's Word on our hearts, it makes those times easier to manage. His Word can guide us through any barrier that confronts us.

Satan and his minions don't want us relying on our Father's words. They often try to manipulate situations to get us to live by the "lust of the flesh, the lust of the eyes, and the pride of life" (1 John 2:16). They don't want us relying on and living by the Spirit. If we live by the Spirit, we can overcome our desire to gratify our sinful nature. One way we depend on the Spirit in this fight against Satan is by carrying God's truth—his Word—within us: "Sanctify them by the truth, your word is truth" (John

17:17). We are made holy by the truth, and the truth is found in the Word of God.

Imagine you have a chest filled with treasures that you've stored away for many years. You have friends who wonder what is inside—perhaps gold, diamonds, and other priceless gems? Imagine their dismay if you open your treasure box and pull out paper clips, rubber bands, buttons, tea bags, and other things of little value. Your friends would think you'd lost your mind.

Our hearts are a treasure box. What treasure are you storing inside for all eternity? Jesus said, "Where your treasure is, there your heart will be also" (Matthew 6:21). Let's make God's Word our treasure. Let's *always* find room to put his Word in our hearts. Let's not be like the Pharisees, whom Jesus called children of the devil because they didn't make room for his words (John 8:37). Few things on this planet are eternal. In fact, I can think of only two: our souls (Romans 6:23) and God's Word (Matthew 24:35). Everything else will disintegrate and burn up. Scriptures we hold within us, will go with us into eternity. We should make it our number one priority to rely on Jesus's words, for they prepare us for spiritual success in this life and in the one to come.

We frequently need to be reminded to keep important what is important. We should never tire of hearing about the value of God's Word. It is like opening a treasure box every day to marvel over the most beautiful gems in the world. In his second letter to Timothy, Paul encouraged him to fight the good fight of faith. He wanted everyone in the faith to finish the race of life with joy no matter the challenge. Paul told Timothy to "keep reminding them of these things" (2 Timothy 2:14). Paul knew God's people needed to be frequently reminded of what is important.

The apostle Peter also frequently reminded the church to keep important what is important. He said, "So I will always remind you of these things, even though you know them and are firmly established in the truth you now have" (2 Peter 1:12). All of us need to be continually urged and prompted to make Scripture our true treasure. Without it, we are like a branch that withers rather than a star that shines brightly as we hold onto the Word of life. This world offers numerous distractions. It is easy to head down a path that leads us far away from reliance on God. Nothing is more important than walking with Him in prayer and Scripture.

Like gold or precious stones that derive their value in part because they are distinct or rare, the Bible is one of a kind. It is a unique book, words from the very breath of God. It has transcended eternity and been dropped into our hands. Montiero-Williams, a former Bowdoin professor of Sanskrit, spent forty-two years studying Eastern books on religions and philosophies. He compared many ancient books of antiquity to the Bible. At the end of his study, he concluded the following:

> Pile them if you will, on the left side of your study table; but place your own Holy Bible on the right side—all by itself, all alone-and with a wide gap between them. For . . . there is a gulf between it and the so-called sacred books of the East which severs the one from the other utterly, hopelessly, and forever.[2]

Let's continue to rely on his Word, for nothing compares with it!

Another reason the Bible is unique is its continuity. In Genesis, we read about the fall of Adam and Eve. God said, "He must not be allowed to reach out his hand and take also from the tree of life and live forever" (Genesis 3:22). The last chapter of Revelation reads, "Blessed are those...that they may have the right to the tree of life and may go through the gates into the city" (Revelation 22:14). In one, paradise is lost; in the other, paradise is regained. In the first, sin separates us from God; in the second, the blood of the Lamb washes away those sins. In the former, we are doomed; in the latter, we are saved. At the fall, Satan is the victor; at the redemption, Jesus crushes him. In the one, death reigns supreme; in the other, life is victorious. Genesis is the end of a sinless life, while Revelation describes the glory of true life in heaven for those who live for Jesus. Genesis is the beginning of God's written Word, while Revelation marks the end. And, of course, a lot of life and history is woven between Genesis and Revelation with amazing continuity.

Sixty-six books comprise the Bible, written over a span of fifteen hundred years by over forty authors who came from every walk of life, including:

- king—David, also a poet
- military leader—Joshua
- fisherman—John
- tax collector—Matthew
- musician—David
- servant—Nehemiah, cupbearer to a pagan king
- herdsmen—Amos
- rabbi—Paul
- doctor—Luke

The Bible was written from different places—Africa, Asia, Europe—and in various settings:

- Jeremiah wrote in a dungeon
- Paul wrote from inside a prison
- John penned Revelation while in exile on the isle of Patmos
- Moses wrote in the wilderness

It was written at different times:

- David, in war
- Solomon, during peace
- Peter, in the midst of the Christians' persecution

In addition, some books were written in different moods: from the depths of sorrow and despair, during days of confusion and doubt, and from the heights of joy. Written in three languages, the books reflect a variety of literary styles:

- poetry
- song
- romance
- satire
- law
- parable
- history
- allegory

Throughout the sixty-six books of Scripture are hundreds of controversial subjects, such as marriage, divorce, sexual impurity, lying, parenting, and more. Yet from Genesis to Revelation is an amazing degree of harmony and consistency. The books' messages are woven into a beautiful, unified tapestry. Try gathering ten people from the same time period, the same town, and with similar interests—you'd be challenged to get them to agree on any controversy. However, the Bible's cohesive message should baffle the mind, considering all the above information. Yet a single, unfolding story or theme that bleeds through its pages is God's love and redemption of humanity. Most important among all the people described in the Bible is the leading character: the one true, living God made known through Jesus Christ.[3]

It's easy to forget how special and unique this wonderful

book is. Too often we take it for granted because we can grab a Bible any time of the day from our bookshelves. We can take it wherever and whenever we want. We can read it silently or aloud in any language. We can read snippets of verses from any of its books. We can listen to the Bible on CD or smartphone. We can pack it with us on a plane, train, or car. We have privileges the early Christians did not. Before the printing press, Scriptures weren't easily accessible. In the early days of the apostles, they had no New Testament to consult. The apostles simply spoke about their experiences with Jesus wherever they traveled. They had the Old Testament, and they were quite adept at relying on it to explain who Jesus was. The apostles and prophets eventually wrote letters to churches to encourage them. It took many years before those letters and gospels came together to form the New Testament.

Can you imagine having only a brief moment to hear one of the gospel letters shared from the pulpit before it was delivered to the next city and another church? How attentive would you be as the words are read? How much of it would you try to memorize, grab hold of, and not let go? I'm not sure how many copies of the epistles or gospels were in existence once the authors penned them. However, we do know that churches shared them with other churches (Colossians 4:16). The members of the Colossae church didn't keep Paul's letter but instead passed it on. We aren't even sure how long the churches held on to certain letters or who had access to them. Maybe they had them for a few days before they were sent off to the next church. Some in the early church memorized large sections of what became Scripture.

Those who memorized the available books of the Bible were known as "living books." Wouldn't you like to be known as a living book? "There goes Frank! He's a living book of Mark's gospel." "Hey, there, Sarah! She's a living book of Ephesians." How encouraging! I have to imagine that a crowd of people followed these living books because they wanted to receive inspiration from God's Word when the written letters or gospels weren't available.[4]

For example, John didn't write his gospel until approximately AD 80 or 90. He is considered to be one of Jesus's most intimate friends—the "disciple whom Jesus loved." He was a part of Jesus's inner circle when the transfiguration took place. Can you imagine spending time with John prior to him writing about his journey with Jesus? I have to believe that many disciples of the first century longed to spend some time with this apostle. He essentially lived with God (Jesus) for three years. Perhaps the early Christians thought, "If only I could sit at his feet and listen to him share about his experiences with Jesus. If only I could hear him tell the story about when Jesus fed the multitude of people with just a few loaves of bread and a couple of fish. Or to hear him share about the shock and dismay of the Pharisees when Jesus called them children of the devil. Or to listen to him share about Jesus's prayer life." We'd have many questions for John about his relationship with Jesus. And yet God has given us the gospel of John, a few snapshots into the heart of John about what his experiences were like when he was around Jesus. Let's be thankful to have God's personal letters to read every day.

The writer of Hebrews wrote about how the prophets of old were despised, rejected, and murdered for preaching God's Word. God knew his chosen ones would be persecuted when speaking boldly and forcefully about how Israel needed to change its ways. The prophet Jeremiah wrote, "I am ridiculed all day long; everyone mocks me. Whenever I speak, I cry out proclaiming violence and destruction. So the word of the LORD has brought me insult and reproach all day long" (Jeremiah 20:8). Hebrews tells about how many of these men and women of God were "stoned, sawed in two, and put to death by the sword. They went about in sheep skins and goatskins; destitute, persecuted and mistreated" (Hebrews 11:37). They were treated that way because they stopped at nothing to be sure God's will was known to the nation of Israel. They cared more about God's honor than they did their lives. They wanted the nation to know how important it was to make God the center of life rather than their superfluous religious laws. These prophets and preachers were more interested in seeking the praise of God rather than the approval of men (John 12:43).

The prophets of old didn't care about earthly treasures; they sought lasting treasure. They were bent on conquest to get to the heavenly city God had prepared for them, and nothing was going to stop them (Hebrews 11:16). Let's be thankful for the treasure the prophets and apostles left behind because they honored God more than they did men.

One way we can show God how much we appreciate his word is by memorizing it. When we commit his word to memory, it can become part of our inner being. When we share it with others from memory, it can come with an authenticity and conviction that springs from deep within our souls. It helps us be more effective at encouraging and inspiring others.

More importantly, imagine the kind of friendship we can develop with God! We speak with God through prayer, and he speaks with us through his Word. Memorizing large sections of Scripture allows us to have deeper conversations with Jesus— anywhere. I recently memorized Psalms 8, 19, 23, 51, 63, 100, and 148. These chapters have moved my heart to praise God like I never have before. They have brought me closer to God. They have shown me the power of God's grace, love, mercy, and magnificence. They have become my heart, because I have etched them there.

We can and must carry his treasure of truth with us always and forever. His truth shines a light on where we fall short and can motivates us to be more like him. I'm glad to know that we have access to the truth at all times. It sets us free from the shackles of guilt and sin.

But what is truth? Where do we find it? How do we know

something is true? These are timeless questions many of us have asked or will ask at some point in our lives. I'm thankful that Jesus brought clarity to the tough questions of life. When we memorize Jesus's words, we find answers to these basic questions of life.

A sad example of someone who had the opportunity to grab hold of truth but let it slip away is Pilate. He was eye to eye with Jesus—Truth personified. However, he was so busy with his job that he missed the chance of a lifetime. He was like many today who are climbing the ladder of success only to get to the top and realize it is leaning against the wrong wall. Don't be that person.

When Pilate was conversing with Jesus in John 18, he asked him, "What is it you have done?" (v. 8). In essence, Pilate asked, "How have you caused all this commotion? What did you do wrong? Why don't they like you? Why are they trying to kill you? Why did they hand you over to me? Why are you not in good favor with them? Who are you anyway? Are you a king?"

"Jesus answered, 'You are right in saying that I'm a king. In fact, for this reason I was born, and for this I came into the world. To testify to the truth. Everyone on the side of truth listens to me'" (v. 37). Then came the question of the ages from Pilate: "What is truth?" (v. 38).

What is truth? What a great question! This governor, who seemingly had it all, had no idea what truth was or where to find it. Unfortunately, he didn't stick around long enough to hear Jesus's answer about where to find truth and how it could impact his life for eternity. Pilate failed to recognize that Truth was in his very presence, and he was about to have him murdered!

When Jesus looked toward heaven and began to pray to the Father, as described in John 17, he gave us the answer of what truth is and where to find it: "Sanctify them by the truth, your word is truth" (v. 17). If we want to know the truth, we need to know God's Word. If we want to be made holy (sanctified), we need to know God's Word. All Scripture is truth. Every word. Every syllable. Even the tough parts we may not understand or fully grasp and agree with. It is all from the heart of God. When you write his Word on your heart, you're planting truth into your life. With truth in your life, you will be more effective at extinguishing the lies of Satan, who will try to discourage, defeat and destroy you.

If you want to uncover the truth about life, the purpose of life, how to build a wonderful marriage, and many other spiritual concepts, dig deeply into to the truth of his Word. When your heart is filled with Scripture, your walk will be more intimate, more affectionate, and deeper with Truth—Jesus, The true treasure (Joh 14:6).

Chapter 2
Walk with God

*I*n the previous chapter, I went into some detail about why God's Word is a treasure we need to carry with us everywhere. It is a book of truth we must never take for granted. This chapter discusses what our walk with God should look like, and demonstrates how memorizing the gospel of John impacted my walk with God. I am confident that whatever portions of Scripture you write on your heart, they will also enrichen your relationship with God.

The Word, Jesus, became flesh. The invisible became visible. The Eternal One entered time and space. The Logos became a baby and grew into a man. The Creator of the universe pitched his tent among us lowly creatures. He wrapped himself with skin, bones, and sinew. Blood coursed through his veins. He was human just like us! Yet he existed with God before time began. He was with the Father before the universe came into existence: "All things were created by him and for him" (Colossians 1:18). He left the comforts of heaven and took on *full humanity*. An astounding concept to ponder. As I think about Jesus growing up, I envision him wrestling with his little brothers and teasing his younger sisters. If he bumped his nose hard enough while jostling around with his brothers, it bled. If he hit his thumb with a hammer, it stung. If he got a splinter, it hurt. If he stubbed his toe, he screamed in agony. If he was made fun of, it made him sad. As a child, when he saw loved ones die it hurt him deeply. He was devastated just like we would be. Jesus didn't just weep in his later years. He felt the sting of sadness throughout his life. Just like us. At times he was disappointed, betrayed, laughed at, ridiculed, and made fun of. He laughed, sang, cried, smiled, frowned, celebrated, loved, and hurt. He had all the experiences of human emotions. Yes, he even got angry on occasion. God identifies with us! We can no longer complain to God by saying, 'but you have no idea what I'm going through.' He knows exactly how we feel!

Jesus also had lots of fun. Hebrews 1:9 says, 'he was anointed with the oil of joy.' Jesus was a happy person. I'm sure there were lively discussions around the dinner table with his parents and siblings. I imagine him spending time with his neighborhood friends, and his brothers tagging along. They probably went swimming in the local lakes, went hiking on trails, climbed mountains, and went fishing. Perhaps they went on many adventurous journeys and camped in the woods. He was like us in every way. He enjoyed the sweet nectar of fruits. He marveled over the snow-capped mountains. He was in awe of the colorful sunsets. He experienced the full gamut of life.

And that is what makes him so special. God *wanted* to become one of us! He *wanted* to feel what it was like to be human. It is one thing to live in the palatial palace of heaven, but a whole different matter to wear flesh and have blood coursing through your veins. I'm sure he must of thought, 'wow, so this is what it is like to be a human.' He was like us in every way, and as a result he can empathize with us during our struggles (Hebrews 2:14; 4:15)

He shows us exactly how we need to live when the troubles of life come and when the good times roll. He sets an example for us on how to deal with overwhelming circumstances. He wants us to see that life is less about what happens to us and more about how we choose to live, no matter what happens! The attitude we choose during the difficult times determines whether or not we live life to the full.

Jesus is our portrait of how life should be lived. He is our role model. He is our mentor, our supreme example to imitate. No one has lived a remarkable life like Jesus. No one even comes close! He is the amazing God-man. Jesus said, "When a man looks at me, he sees the one who sent me . . . I and the Father are one" (John 12:44; 10:30). He spoke these words to the crowd that followed him, and they knew exactly what Jesus meant when he said those words—that he is God. They picked up stones on two occasions to kill him. They were ticked off that a man had uttered such preposterous words: "I and the Father are one."

Earlier in the gospel, Jesus was nearly stoned to death because he said, "Before Abraham was born, I am" (John 8:58). He was, of course, referring to the encounter God had with Moses at the burning bush in Exodus. In fact, Jesus was saying he was *The I am* who interacted with Moses at the bush. He was emphatically stating that he existed before Abraham, Moses, and all the greats of old. The Jews were stunned. "How could a guy like this make such claims? We know his father, mother, and siblings— they're common folk. He's from the lowly town of Nazareth. Is he seriously saying he is God?" The Jews became angry and picked up stones to murder this man because of blasphemy!

> Jesus looked at them and said, "I have shown you many great miracles from the Father. For which of these do you stone me?" "We are not stoning you for any of these replied the Jews, but for blasphemy, because you a mere man claim to be God. (John 10:32–33)

Sadly, they didn't believe he was God so they prepared to kill the God whom they worshipped and took great pride in. How their disbelief must have pained the Father's heart.

Why were they so insistent on putting Jesus to death? He was an ordinary man who lived an extraordinary life of love and concern for others. He wasn't flashy. He didn't live in a palace. He wasn't formally educated by rabbis. He wasn't clothed in the finest robes. In fact, he had no place to lay his head (Luke 9:29). The Jews refused to believe that the One who had said, "Let there be light . . . let there be an expanse ... let the water teem . . . let us make man in our image" was standing before them.

The Jews rejected Jesus, the Word of God, who had brought the entire universe into existence. They were repulsed by him. Why did they hate him so much? Why did so many people turn against him? His mom and siblings thought he was crazy. Even his own brothers made fun of him. They ridiculed and teased him thinking he was showboat. They prodded him to go to Jerusalem to make a display of his miracles to the world. He responded to their critical spirit by telling them, "For you any time is right. The world cannot hate you, but it hates me, because I testify that what it does is evil" (John 7:6–7). The Jews wanted to put him to death because he shook their belief system to the core. How could God become a man? They were angry about Jesus performing many of his miracles on the Sabbath. Here was this man bringing hope and healing to people, and because it was done on a particular day, the Jews despised him. They hated him! He was a light shining in a very dark world. His life was so brilliant that it blinded people. Many wanted nothing to do with him. However, he didn't shrink back. He shined so brightly that not even the darkness of death could contain him.

As his disciples, we have the privilege of building a relationship with this magnificent person. What an honor! But we can be easily distracted from spending time with Jesus. Yet nothing is more important than our daily walk with him. In John 15:4, he said, "Apart from me you can do nothing." What does nothing mean? It means not a thing. We can't do anything unless we remain in Jesus. Of course he is referring to our spiritual lives. If we want to please him, we must go to him. In Romans 8:8, Paul says, "Those controlled by the sinful nature cannot please God." If we do not remain, abide, and depend on Jesus and his word for our source of strength, we will eventually end up becoming a withered branch to be tossed away and burned.

We may think we're doing okay without remaining in him, but that's merely our flesh living an okay life without Jesus at the center. We deceive ourselves if we think we can live a righteous life without abiding in him (Philippians 1:11). We may even have an appearance of bearing the good fruits of love, joy, peace, patience, etc...but unless we are getting fed spiritually through our walk with Jesus, unless we are depending on his word, unless we are relying on him, we will wither.

We may be successful at our jobs, have a good marriage, have decent friendships, be somewhat content, and make lots of money; but Jesus isn't talking about those things. We can gain the whole world, *but unless Jesus is our life*, what do we have? Nothing! We must walk as he walked (1 John 2:6). How can we walk as Jesus walked if we aren't constantly yearning to learn how he walked? And how can we ponder how he walked if we aren't examining Scripture? We must open up the pages of the Bible to gain precious insights into the life of Jesus. Once we understand how he lived, then *we must put it into practice*. It is then that we will thrive, be fruitful, and prove ourselves to be his disciples (John 15:8).

If we don't strive to live like him during our time on earth, how do we expect to live with him in the next life? "Now this is eternal life: that they may know you the only true God, and Jesus Christ whom you have sent" (John 17:2). Almost everyone wants eternal life when they die. Even the most hardened criminals. However, if we make no effort in getting to know eternal life (Jesus) while alive, how can we possibly think we'll be with God in heaven if we spend little to no time getting to know him on earth? Impossible! Jesus demands us to make every effort to enter through the narrow door (Luke 13:24). We can't ignore our relationship with God while on earth and then think we'll enter heaven when we die. On the flip side, what a blessing to experience a little taste of eternity on earth by getting to know both the Father and Jesus while we are alive! When we die, it seamlessly continues.

A major reason I strove to memorize Scripture, and especially the gospel of John, was that I wanted to know Jesus. I didn't merely want to know *about* him; I wanted to know him deeply, intimately. It's nice to know about where he was born, where he traveled, and who he interacted with during his earthly ministry. It's good to know who his twelve apostles were. However, those are merely facts. We should strive to know his heart and character. What motivated him? What was his prayer life like? How did he shower the Father with love, praise, and adoration? How did he please the Father? What did he say to the Father? How did he demonstrate his love for others?

I also wanted to know why Jesus loved me, a wretched sinner. I memorized this gospel because John does a masterful job of painting a beautiful picture of who Jesus was in the flesh. We catch a glimpse of the heart of God in action. We see him cry, we see him thirst, and we see him tire. We also witness him forgive and receive worship (John 9:38 See Chapter 8). We see how he masterfully reasoned with an angry crowd about to kill a woman caught in adultery. The *only sinless One* who could have thrown the stones, did not; instead, he displayed love, grace and mercy.

The gospel of John has provided me with numerous nuggets of wisdom about the heart and character of Jesus. My spiritual life has been rejuvenated often over the years because of the words found in the fourth gospel. I'm certain memorization of Scripture can do the same for you.

John's gospel has been an anchor for my soul, a continuous source of strength for my faith. Whenever I begin to drift from

God because of sin, I merely whisper words from this gospel and the embers of my heart begin to flicker and soften once again.

Reading the Bible is essential, and studying it is better, but *memorizing it is best of all.* When we write his Word on our hearts they breathe spiritual life into us (John 6:63). They create a greater personal connection with him. They give us a better chance of remaining firmly in the vine. "If you remain in me, and my words remain in you, ask whatever you wish and it will be given you" (John 15:5). He will give us more than we can ask or imagine—spiritually, our relationship with Jesus will grow closer and deeper when his word remains in us.

Let's have a little fun with our imaginations. This may never be true in our lifetimes but no one knows the future, so imagine you're asked to take a solo mission to North Korea. Kim Jong-un is a tyrannical dictator, who has no trust in his leaders. He kills anyone who mentions anything resembling opposition. The country has no religious freedom. In fact, the people have no freedoms of any kind. For example, you can't meet publicly with other Christians. You can't high-five a brother and sister about having a great quiet time. No conferences are available to attend where you can hear sermons. You can't grab a morning coffee at Starbucks and enjoy some fellowship with a member of the church. No public display of spiritual encouragement with a child of God is allowed. You cannot lift your voice up in song to God in public, unless, of course, you want to be imprisoned. In fact, you are forbidden to do that even in the privacy of your own home. If you breathe even a hint of being a Christian, you'll disappear, never to be heard from again. Although the following excerpt is from an article published in 2011, it is still true today—probably even more so!

According to an article found in Listverse, North Korea is the most dangerous country in the world for Christians.

North Korea's persecution of Christians knows no equal, and being a Christian there is considered one of the worst crimes possible. North Korean communist dogma considers religion an "opiate" of the people, unless of course that religion is the personality cult of the 'Great Leader' Kim II Sung or his son, 'Dear Leader' Kim Jong II. North Korean Christians must hide their faith at all times, and Christian parents can't teach their faith to their children until the kids are old enough to understand the dangers—and to be sure their kids won't turn them in. Just owning a Bible in North Korea is grounds for execution or deportment to a harsh labor camp (essentially a gulag). Despite the risks, the Christian church is growing: an estimated 400,000 believers now sing silent hymns in cramped basements of crumbling buildings.[1]

It's hard to believe there are still places in the world where simply owning a Bible is grounds for execution. Imagine that your only desire is to read a book that communicates thoughts about God and how to live a better life, but you are forbidden to do so.

You may never be asked to go on a mission to North Korea; however, what if you were? How would you fare if you were imprisoned where Bibles aren't allowed? What if you didn't know anyone? Would you thrive in your walk with God or wither from bitterness? Would your prayer life grow or die? Would you be filled with greater faith or filled with skepticism and doubt? Since Scripture is a vital part of your walk with God, what parts of the Bible could you recite to keep your mind focused on things above? What verses would you share with those who may be interested in learning about Jesus? What kind of quiet times would you have in your prison cell with no Bible to read? What if we were asked to recite Scripture for an underground church so they can write it down? What passages could you share?

I've often thought about being called by God to go to a country like this. It is almost as though people in these places are living lives similar to those the first-century Christians, where scant copies of the apostles' letters were passed around from church to church. Wouldn't it be incredible to be asked to go to a place like that to secretly share a book you've memorized so someone could write it down and then bring them closer to Jesus? How inspiring would it be to get a call to help God's church in this way! What scriptures would you share with them? Do you know those passages word for word?

We take for granted the freedoms we enjoy in the United States. As much as President Trump may want to make America great again, it may not happen. We may not always enjoy the freedoms we have today. What if North Korea conquered America and made Christianity illegal overnight? What if they made carrying a Bible illegal? What if they destroyed all Bibles and passed a law that made it a crime to be caught with one, leading to the death penalty for you and your children? What selections from Scripture are burned onto your heart?

Let's always cherish the words God gave us. He went through so much to give us his inspired Word. Lives have been lost so we could have his Word near us at all times.

I encourage you to start memorizing. Once you've memorize a few verses, memorize several more. Your walk with God can thrive in all situations when you write his Word on your heart. Paul admonished the church in Colossae, "Let the word of Christ dwell in you richly" (Colossians 3:10). The word dwell means *"to live in."* In other words, when you memorize Scripture, you are making a home in your heart for God's Word. You carry it with you wherever you go, because it lives in you. The Word should richly, or abundantly, be in all believers. If you focus intently on having his words living in you, it will help you to change, grow, and develop a more intimate relationship with him. It will strengthen you in your fight against sin. It will keep your mind focused on things above, not on earthly things.

Deuteronomy 6:6–9 says:

> These commandments that I give you today are to be upon your hearts. Impress them on your children. Talk about them when you sit at home and when you walk along the road, when you lie down and when you get up. Tie them as symbols on your hands and bind them on your foreheads. Write them on the door frames of your houses and on your gates.

If you've been around the church for more than a few days, you've probably heard this scripture spoken of more than once. A lot of people talk about how important it is to be in the Word; however, we need to have the Word in us—in our souls, written on our hearts, and etched on our brains.

A scripture that astounds me is Amos 8:11, in which God said through the prophet:

> The days are coming, declares the Sovereign LORD, when I will send a famine through the land—not a famine of food or thirst for water, but a famine of hearing the word of the LORD. Men will stagger from sea to sea and wander from North to East, searching for the word of the LORD, but they will not find it.

Imagine not being able to find a Bible anywhere. You search everywhere for just one copy, and you can't find any. What a horrifying thought! God told his people that this would be their reality at some point. The good news for us is that the Bible is the number 1 best-selling book every year. You can find a copy almost anywhere. However, there are times when you'll not have your Bible with you, but you can always have the words of God in you. When Satan tempted Jesus in the desert, did Jesus pull out a scroll and tell Satan, "Hold on. I need to find a passage in the Old Testament to combat your deception"? Did Satan read from a scroll when he tempted Jesus? Of course not. Satan knew exactly what passages to use in his attempt to get Jesus to stumble. He tried to trick Jesus using Scripture, and he failed because Jesus fought back with God's Word. Jesus was prepared to do battle against the evil one! Satan used the same deceptive practice on Eve in the garden: "Did God really say …?" (Genesis 2:8). Unfortunately, unlike Jesus, Eve and Adam didn't hold firm to God's command. Satan won the battle that day, and it changed the course of human history.

I thoroughly enjoy being able to take God's Word wherever I go, and I don't necessarily mean in book form or digitally, though I'm thankful for all the ways the Bible is available. I travel quite a bit as an account executive. A while back I was at the Charlotte airport. I had a long layover, and I wanted to have a quiet time with God. Charlotte's airport is always very busy. I tried to find an area with no distractions but there was none to be found. So, I put on my headset and pretended I was talking with someone on the phone, but I was talking with God by reciting out loud a few chapters of John. In the midst of all the hustle and bustle, I was walking with God and gaining fresh insight into the heart and life of Jesus. In the middle of all the craziness, he and I were building our friendship. Isn't it good to know that we can deepen our friendship with God wherever we go? When we etch Scripture on our hearts, we can intimately reflect on, rely on, and call on God anywhere at any time.

Let me encourage you to memorize one of your favorite chapters of a gospel. The gospels give amazing detail about Jesus's life. Pick a chapter and go over it continuously until the words sink deep into your memory. Recite the words wherever you go for a couple months. (Later I'll share some strategies on how to memorize.)

Think about the words every day. Meditate on them. Share them with a friend or family member. Use them in your prayer life. As you pour over the words, your desire to spend time with Jesus will increase. You'll have a greater motivation to walk as Jesus walked. You'll always be learning something new about Jesus. Let's be like Paul, who was laser focused on learning all he could about Jesus. He considered everything he owned and all he had accomplished as rubbish compared with the surpassing greatness of knowing Jesus (Philippians 3:9). He wanted to know him as a friend. Doesn't it inspire you when you read, "Abraham was called God's friend" (James 2:23)? God also called Moses his friend: "The LORD would speak with Moses face to face, as a man speaks with his friend" (Exodus 33:11). Of course, these men didn't see God fully realized because no one could have done that and lived. Face-to-face simply means they shared a close relationship with God.

Imagine if Jesus whispered in your ear, "Thanks for being such a good friend to me." It's possible for us to be God's friend. Memorizing enhances that quest. Jesus told his disciples, "I no longer call you servants, because a servant does not know his master's business. Instead I have called you friends, for everything that I've learned from my father I have made known to you" (John 15:15). Let's continue to strive to build a deeper walk with Jesus by holding on to his word.

The Word is living; it transcends time. What was written thousands of years ago still applies to us today. Times may have changed, cultures may have changed, but Jesus is still at work in our lives at this very moment. He said, "My Father is always at his work, and I too am working" (5:17). God never stops being involved in our lives. What Jesus said to the twelve can be true of us! We can be his friends. When the day arrives for me to be with

God, I hope he will say, "Thank you for being my good friend." May he say the same about you, too.

God challenges us to "keep my commands . . . bind them on your fingers; write them on the tablet of your heart" (Proverbs 7:2–3). How do we write his commands on our hearts? I wish it were as easy as writing words on paper or as simple as typing words into a document. Unfortunately, it requires focus and lots of repetition. The words must be forged on the heart by time, effort, and discipline. As you know, you reap what you sow (Galatians 6:7). You will reap a harvest of greater closeness with your Maker if you give your heart to this practice.

If you want to be a good pianist, run a marathon, lose weight, be a great golfer or gamer, what must you do? It takes lots of time and practice repeated often. If you want to write God's Word on your heart, it will take lots discipline and practice. Satan wants disciples to neglect scripture so they will have no weapon to use in defense against his constant onslaughts. No matter how vehemently Christians may claim to believe the Bible from cover to cover, if it's not used, it's useless. His word is food for life. It sustains us. If we don't eat, we don't live. If we have no water, we'll die within days. Jesus told the woman by the well about water that forever quenches spiritual thirst and gives eternal life. He told her, "Everyone who drinks this water will be thirsty again, but whoever drinks the water I give him will never thirst. Indeed, the water I give him will become in him a spring of water welling up to eternal life" (John 4:13). In Deuteronomy 8:3, God also said, "Man does not live on bread alone, but on every word that comes from the mouth of the LORD."

Let's regularly feast on his words. The more we embrace them, the more motivated we'll be to worship him. We worship God when we shower him with adoration, reverence, and praise. It's our spiritual act of devotion. He lavishes us with mercy and grace, with blessings and favor. He forgives us when we don't deserve it. "You will again have compassion on us; you will tread our sins underfoot and hurl all our iniquities into the depths of the sea" (Micah 7:19). Although I may go back to fish for my sins in order to remind myself what a wretched man I am, God forgets them forever! It is his promise. Let's claim it! Our hearts should overflow with gratitude and praise as we think about how much God loves us.

Have you ever felt that God has abandoned you or doesn't love you? You may wrestle with such thoughts when you're enduring challenging times. You may feel overwhelmed and hopeless. However, there is no reason to doubt God's love for you. Jesus didn't doubt God loved him, even when his body was crushed by the power of the scourge and his best friends claimed not to know him. As his hands and feet were impaled on the beams of wood, he never let go of the Father's love. We need to hold on to this same attitude. We need to worship God in good times and bad, when we are succeeding or failing, whether we are well fed or hungry, when life is easy or hard, when we are rich or poor, and whether we are living in plenty or in want.

Jesus said, "True worshipers will worship the Father in spirit and truth, for they are the kind the worshipers the Father seeks" (John 4:23). God is searching for true worshippers, and he specifically shares what is required to make him happy in our devotion to him. If we want to please him in our personal worship, we need to follow his blueprint found in Scripture. (Emphasis mine). Jesus said, *"The words* I have spoken to you *are Spirit* and they are life" (6:63). In another place Jesus said, "Sanctify them by the truth, *your word is truth"* (17:17). Here are a couple of instances where Jesus said we find Spirit and truth in his words. The psalmist wrote, "All your words are true; all your righteous laws are eternal" (Psalm 119:160).

If we want to worship God acceptably, as described by Jesus, we certainly need his Holy Spirit within; but we must also have his Word with us. Read, ponder, and obey the truth—his Word. Meditate on it day and night.

Let's put more of his Word within us, as we seek the praise of our Father in worship (John 5:44). It is true, we not only give praise to God, but we also receive praise in return from him! Let's grab hold of the scriptures and never let them go.

Chapter 3
Walk by Prayer

*D*o you ever feel you can't pray for more than a few minutes without being distracted? Have you ever prayed for a while and when finished, you asked yourself, was it the air or God I was speaking with? This has occurred to me more times than I care to admit.

As Christ followers, we should experience a closeness with Jesus that moves us to want more of him. On many occasions, I've spent a good deal of time with him in prayer but all I did was ask him for things. There's nothing wrong with asking God for blessings; however, God expects more from us than merely making requests of him. Think of your friends or family members; how would you feel if all they did was ask you for things whenever you get together? Or if all they talked about was themselves? My three children are quite adept at asking for stuff. At times, I'm happy to give, but at other times, I ask, "Why do you need yet another . . . ?"

But Jesus did say, "Ask you and you will receive, knock and the door will be open to you" (Matthew 7:7). What should be our most important desire when spending time with God? We need to be sure we're asking Jesus to give us what the Spirit desires. "This is the confidence we have in approaching God: that if we ask anything according to his will, he hears" (I John 5:21). Do we ask Jesus to show us how we can be a better friend to him? Do we ask him to show us how we can be more pleasing to him? Are we begging him to give us a better understanding of his heart, life, and character? Our lives should be consumed with getting to know Jesus.

My children ask me, "Dad, can we talk? I have something heavy on my heart," or "Dad, can I get your guidance on an idea I have?" Or maybe they simply say, "I love you because . . ." What parent doesn't long to hear those words from his or her children? Do you think God is any different? He longs to hear us say, "Abba, Father." He wants us to be so intimate with him that we freely and confidently call him Papa. This concept is hard for many of us to embrace, but it's a fact! He is our dad, our papa. He loves us like a father, but he's also firm like one too. He is also gentle and nurturing like a mother. We may not have had the best dad or mom growing up. Perhaps your mom or dad was absent from your life. Thankfully we have Scripture to give us a perfect understanding of what a father and mother should be like. God perfectly represents both mother and father. There is no one who reveals beautiful details about the Father quite like Jesus. The both of them desire to build a home within each of us (John 14:23). Wow!

Imagine strolling along a beach, climbing a mountain, walking along your favorite path, or driving for hours in your car and you begin talking with God by reciting Jesus's prayer in John 17. I've done that on more than one occasion. It always moves my heart. I've prayed through the twenty-one chapters of John many times. I'm astounded at the new insights I gain into the life of Jesus. I also gain a better understanding of my own heart.

John 17 gives us a totally different perspective on what our relationship with the Father in prayer should be like. Listen to these words from Jesus's prayer in John 17: "Father, I want those you have given me to be with me where I am and to see my glory, the glory you have given me because you loved before the creation of the world" (v. 24). What a special prayer Jesus offered up to the Father on our behalf! He prayed for you. He prayed for me. He prayed to the Father for us to see him in heaven. I can read these words and breeze over them without understanding their full meaning. When I meditate on these words from memory, I am able to better capture the essence of Jesus's prayer life. It helps me to imitate the kind of walk he had with the Father. I gain a deeper understanding of what was vitally important to Jesus in prayer: He didn't pray for things. He prayed for hearts—yours and mine—to be moved closer to God!

As our prayer life grows and we become more connected with God, we should naturally let others know how we are being transformed—boasting about what God is doing! Isn't it a natural part of relationships to update one another with what's going on in our lives? We should do the same with Jesus. What do we boast about most in our lives? Athletic accomplishments? How much money we make? The college we attended? Making the dean's list? The clothes we wear, the neighborhood we live in, or the car we drive (or want)? What do we boast about in the quietness of our hearts?

Let's look at what God says we should boast about: "Let not the wise man boast of his wisdom or the strong man boast of his strength or the rich man boast of his riches, but let him who boasts boast about this: that he understands and knows me" (Jeremiah 9:23). Do we boast about getting to know God more every day? Believers' greatest longing in life should be to know him more. Paul said he desired to boast in nothing except in the cross of Jesus Christ (Galatians 6:14). What are we boasting about in our conversations with other disciples? Hopefully we are focused on inspiring each other to grow in our love for God.

I recently decided that when I wake up at around 5:30 a.m., I will head straight for the sanctuary I've created—my enclosed porch. On a table sits a little lantern. And over the lantern I have placed a hat with the words JESUS IS HERE stitched on it. When

I turn on the lantern, Jesus is here is illuminated. I had a sign made from scrap wood with the words, 'The Lord is with you, when you are with him (2 Chronicles 15:2). Every morning I look forward to spending at least an hour with God in prayer. I used to get up and grab my iPhone, iPad, or computer to check my emails. One email would lead to ten, and then I'd browse the Internet. Before I knew it, a couple hours had passed by, and it was time to begin my work day.

Now when I get up, I feed the dogs, get my tea, and I head to my sanctuary. At times I've been tempted to pick up the phone between making tea and feeding the dogs, but I know my weakness, so I avoid electronics at all cost. I imagine them being a black hole that will suck me in. My walk with God is too important to be distracted from it.

Jesus gives us many promises to latch on to. One of which is that when we find him, he will never let us go. Once he has us in his hand, nothing will ever be able to come between us and him. "No one can snatch them out of my hand" (John 10:28). We can choose to drift from him, but he will always be at the door of our hearts knocking to let him in. Paul echoed these words in Romans 8:37:

> For I am convinced that neither death nor life, neither the angles nor demons, neither the present nor the future, nor any powers, neither height nor depth, nor anything else in all creation, will be able to separate us from the love of God that is in Christ Jesus our Lord.

If you are in Christ (see chapter 12), you can live confident of God's unconditional love. Only one thing can destroy our relationship with God—turning away from him and going back to the world (1 John 2:15).

The writer of Hebrews said, "Anyone who comes to him,

must believe that he exists and that he rewards those who earnest seek him" (Hebrews 11:6). Another scripture in Psalm 19:11 says, "...in keeping them there is great reward." In keeping his commands, statutes, precepts, law, etc...there is great *reward*. Let's be honest, most people love rewards. They make us happy. If you're like me, you want your employer to reward you for your hard work—preferably in the form of a bonus. Your reward for being a successful parent is your children acting respectfully and responsibly. I'm sure we can come up a litany of rewards we'd like to have.

One reward far exceeds anything we can imagine, but a lot of us miss it. Oftentimes I miss it because I get caught up in the busyness of life. The greatest reward we receive by seeking God with all our heart, mind, soul and strength is . . . drumroll . . . *God!* In Genesis 15:1, when God was about to make his covenant with Abraham, he told him, "Do not be afraid . . . *I AM* your very great reward." All other rewards we chase after pale in comparison to nurturing an intimate walk with God. There should be no greater reward we seek than knowing him.

When we lose sight of making God number one in our lives, we risk spiraling down to a dark place very quickly. *Even as disciples* we can feel hopeless or discouraged or even depressed when we don't invest our time, heart, and focus into our walk with God. We start filling our lives with shallow and empty things. Having our hearts filled with his Word reminds us of why we need to rely on him daily. Life is hopeless without a relationship with God.

A few years ago, I had a friend who had a wonderful family. They lived in a big home, had two nice cars, a Harley, and many other such toys I admired. At one point he boasted about having a million dollars of what he called "play money" that he'd invested in the stock market. He also left his corporate job and bought a small business. The family seemed happy and content. *Man, this guy has everything*, I thought. I was intimidated about sharing God with him.

However, a year or so later, his stocks crashed, his business floundered, and his money was gone. It happened overnight. Satan was on the prowl, looking for someone to devour. My neighbor lost everything, from a material point of view, and it crushed his spirit.

Not long after all of this happened, the news came that while visiting his parent's home, he'd taken his life. The community was devastated. His wife later told me that he had taken his life so his family could get the benefits from his life insurance policy. He filled his life with things, but what he needed was God, who would love him, be with him, and fill his life in a way no amount of money or possessions can. My heart ached for him and his family. This memory still haunts me. I truly believe that if he'd known Jesus, I'd be telling a different story.

I often tell my children to imagine their hearts as the shape of a door with a lock, and only one key will open it. Many keys may fit, but they fail to unlock it. Keys such as money, fame, relationships, career, possessions, family, etc., seem to fit, but none of them can unlock the door. Perhaps some of the keys provide temporary satisfaction. However, only one key can open the door and satisfy their hearts with everlasting freedom, satisfaction, and fulfillment: a relationship with Jesus! He is the key who can unlock the door of our hearts. He is the only one who can make our lives full.

Over the last several years, we have witnessed the deaths of several music icons. They seemingly had everything: fame, popularity, money, cars, houses, and more. They didn't lack for anything, yet they either took their own lives or died of a drug overdose. It appears they were looking for life and fulfillment in the wrong places. No person or thing can ever stand in the place of Jesus. Only he can complete us. Elvis Presley is one of the most well-known singers who ever lived. He, too, had the world at his fingertips, yet he was very unhappy with his life. David Stanley, his stepbrother, was asked why Elvis took destructive drugs that ultimately lead to his death. Stanley answered by quoting Elvis, "I would rather be unconscious than miserable."[1] Life is empty without God!

Another great success story is Winston Churchill. *Time Magazine* chose him as 'Man of the Half-Century' (1900–1950), and in 2002 BBC viewers voted him the greatest man of Great Britain. Yet listen to Churchill's own words as he reflected on his life: "I have achieved a great deal to achieve nothing in the end."[2] Many people are crying for help, but without Jesus in their lives, none will be found! *God must be their lives,* or they will never have the peace that passes understanding, no matter what they fill their lives with (Colossians 3:4). It's hard enough to fight the battle of life with God *in us,* never mind trying to do it without him.

I'm not throwing stones at these famous people. We are all empty without Jesus. He is the key to the heart!

One of the wisest men who ever lived was Solomon. He, too, filled his life with people and things. But in the end, he described it as a chasing after the wind. "Meaningless! Meaningless! Everything is meaningless!" (Ecclesiastes 12:8). You can hear the desperation in his words plastered throughout this book's pages. He concludes the book by challenging us to make God the center of our lives. "Now all has been heard; here is the conclusion of the matter: Fear God and keep his commandments, for this is the whole duty of man" (v. 13). In the end, the only thing that mattered to Solomon was God.

Within each person is a longing for things eternal. We can try to squelch, squash, and push it away, but in the end, *there God is.* In his God-given wisdom, Solomon said, "God has set eternity in the hearts of men" (Ecclesiastes 3:11). He wants to fill us with eternal life, so why not let him? Let's walk with him in prayer and get a taste of eternity on earth.

One of my favorite things to do in my prayer life is to talk out loud with God, reciting the chapters and books I've memorized. It doesn't matter where I am. Praying Scripture puts me into a state of awareness that Jesus is with me, he is speaking with me. I often travel five hours by car to Atlanta, where my corporate office is. As much as I hate navigating Atlanta traffic, I look forward to those journeys; it means I get five hours of alone time with God. No distractions. No kids screaming for my attention. No demands. Just me and God. It's my mountaintop time when I leave everything behind and center my thoughts on Jesus. I pray the scriptures I've memorized. At times, I'm moved to tears as I think about Jesus in the various scenes portrayed in the gospel of John. Other times, I'm inspired by Paul's faithfulness, even though he faced epic challenges. Sometime I cry when I think about David's brokenness described in Psalm 51. Though I've recited these selections thousands of times, they never get old. God's Word is timeless. It always breathes life into my walk with God.

On a recent trip to Atlanta, I wanted to see how long it would take me to recite all the scriptures I've memorized over the years—approximately 20,000 words. It took five hours. I began reciting as soon as I left my home, and finished when I arrived at my hotel.

Nothing makes my heart leap for joy more than pondering Jesus's life. It has been a twenty-three-year journey with the gospel of John. There's always a feast to be had when walking and talking with Jesus through this gospel. The words of this book help me to build a deeper friendship with him. As I recite John's words they move me to adore and thank him for his goodness, mercy, and graciousness.

Think of your best friend. Why is he or she your best friend? Building a friendship is not easy; it takes a lot of work and time. You create special memories by being open about your lives. You understand each other, have fun together. A friendship with anyone requires focus, effort, and energy. Building a friendship with God is no different; it requires time. Lots of time. It's so simple that it's difficult. Not because God has made it difficult; rather, we have. We're easily distracted. We let worries, responsibilities, and the cares of this world consume our time. We barely give God the leftovers. And then we wonder why we aren't close to him.

One of my favorite stories about how simple it is to build an intimate prayer life with God is found in Luke 10:37.

> As Jesus and his disciples were on their way, he came to a village where a woman named Martha opened her home to him. She had a sister called Mary, who sat at the Lord's feet listening to what he said. But Martha was distracted by all the preparations that had to be made. She came to him and asked, "Lord, don't you care that my sister has left me to do the work by myself? Tell her to help me!"
>
> "Martha, Martha," the Lord answered, "You are worried and upset about many things, but only one thing is needed. Mary has chosen what is better, and it will not be taken away from her."

I can relate to Martha. It's easy to be distracted by the world. Jesus knows this because he knows us. He understands us because he became one of us. He knows of the many things that put demands on our time, energy, and focus, but only one thing is needed in our spiritual lives: sitting at his feet. Martha missed it. Mary got it! Jesus was not going to take away this special connection from her! How much time do we spend watching TV, shopping, and tinkering on our smart devices? We need to be like Mary, who chose to sit at Jesus's feet and just listen to him. She marveled at this great and humble man. You don't have to be a multitalented person to be a friend of Jesus. You don't need to be rich, a leader, have a degree from a prestigious institution, or live a perfect life for Jesus to be your friend. We simply need to *invest our time* with him.

We all need a special place where we can close the door and be alone with God, where we quiet our souls, sit at his feet, and talk with him (1 Chronicles 17:16). As I mentioned earlier, the porch has become my place to meet with God. During this time, I go through an acronym called ACTS: Adore, Confess, Thankfulness, and Supplication.[3] ACTS helps me stay focused on how to praise, confess, and pray for myself and others. I also need to be thankful for all the ways God has blessed me. "From the fullness of his grace we have all received one blessing after another" (John 1:16). Interwoven throughout my time of prayer, I converse with God, reciting chapters of Scripture from memory. I also continue to memorize various psalms because they help me put ACTS into action. I invite you to apply this same concept in your time with the Lord.

When you have his words in you, you'll be able to shut your eyes, meditate, ponder, contemplate, and pray more intimately. Find that special place where you can be alone with Him and put ACTS into action. Your relationship with Jesus will become more special.

Chapter 4
Walk by Meditation

A book I enjoy reading is *Beyond Survival* by Gerald Coffee.[1] It's about his seven-year ordeal as a prisoner of war in Vietnam. He was an Air Force pilot whose plane had been hit by artillery. He and his copilot flew as far as they could from enemy territory, but eventually they had to ditch the plane. They ejected and parachuted into the ocean. His copilot died before they could reach land. The Viet Cong captured Coffee. His seven years of hell on earth began.

When they brought him to a village, the people kicked, punched, and spat on him. They blamed him for the death of their loved ones. They wanted to kill him, but the Viet Cong wanted him alive to get information from him.

He spent harrowing years in prison in the infamous Hanoi Hilton. Brutally beaten, he suffered much and had very little to no physical contact with other captives in the prison, who lived in six-by-four-foot cells barely big enough for them. The Viet Cong understood the value of social interaction. If these prisoners were caught talking to one another, they would be mercilessly beaten. They knew if they could isolate the captured soldiers, their chances of breaking down the men and getting secret information increased.

The prisoners devised a code to "talk" with one another. The system involved an alphabet structure that allowed the soldiers to communicate through tapping on walls, sweeping floors, coughing, etc...It was astounding how much information they shared using this method. They learned languages, "recited" poetry, told jokes, shared stories, and quoted Scripture. No verbal communication. Human ingenuity at its best.

What if you had been a prisoner in one of those cells? What if you wanted to encourage your fellow captives? What passages could you share? Imagine tapping one of your favorite psalms through the walls. The chances are pretty slim any of us will wind up in a Viet Cong prison, but many times we feel like prisoners in our cars when we're stuck in traffic. Maybe we feel trapped in our cubicles at work. Having his Word readily available within can transform mundane situations into glorious opportunities to grow closer to God and to encourage others.

Meditation is a critical step in helping us mold his words in our memory. For Scripture to be in you, it requires spending a fair amount of time reciting and meditating on it. The word *meditation* has been hijacked by Eastern mysticism. It's not some hocus-pocus magic spell you put over yourself. The Hebrew words for meditation are *haga* and *sihach*. They are used thirty-eight times in Psalms. Meditation is more than thinking and reflecting on the Word. It also carries the idea of talking, uttering, murmuring, speaking, complaining, conversing, crying out, communing, declaring, praying, and praising. It is focusing your mind on the words you have planted within you. Meditation is a process of prayerful uttering on the rich meaning of Scripture. When you meditate, you are concentrating on and being unhurried in your thoughts on God's Word.

Protect at all costs the verses and books you work hard to memorize. Hold them captive within you. Do not allow the rich treasures of God's Word to be washed away from your mind by the worries of this world. Do not let the demands of life, no matter how important, push aside his Word. Meditating on scripture will fortify your mind against Satan's attacks.

The word *katecho* in Luke 8:15 carries the idea of keeping something in memory: "Those who hear the word, *retain it*, and by persevering produce a crop." Retaining the Word takes practice; it requires consistent meditation. In 1 Corinthians 15:2, Paul wrote, "By this gospel you are saved, if you hold firmly to the word." "Holding firmly" is the translation of *katecho*.

When you frequently meditate on Scripture, it becomes easier to retain, and over time the words are planted like a tree with deep roots in your life. According to www.definition.com, the word *retain* means, "keep possession of; not discard; keep in one's memory." It is imperative to figure out a way to retain or keep possession of God's Word. In his letter to the Romans, Paul was emphatic about the importance of retaining the Word of God. He confirmed that it will help us to be pure in a world filled with depravity and evil. "Furthermore, since they did not think it worthwhile to *retain* the knowledge of God, he gave them over to a depraved mind, to do what ought not to be done" (Romans 1:28 emphasis mine).

When you fill your life with Scripture through retention, you make better decisions to live as God commands. We will be happier no matter the circumstances that come our way! And most important, our Father will smile at the good heart we are developing. Let's read those words again in Luke 8:15, "But the seed on good soil stands for those with a noble and good heart, who hear the word, *retain it,* and by persevering produce a crop." What portions of Scripture will you retain to produce a crop? God wants to see the fruit of your life. He wants to see results. Let's retain his Word so that we are pleasing to him.

Meditation is part of the process of firmly fixing Jesus's words within us, to avoid drifting away from him. It doesn't take long for us to feel distant from God when we stop praying and relying on his Word. Meditation is one way to stay on track. Psalm 119 has some of the best thoughts about the importance of meditation.

My eyes stay open through the watches of the
night that I may meditate on your promises . . .
Oh how I love your law! I meditate on it all day
long . . . I have more insight than all my teachers for
I meditate on your statues . . . Let me understand
the teaching of your precepts, then I will meditate
on your wonder. (vv. 148, 97, 99, 27)

The Lord challenged Joshua to grab hold of and never let go
of Scripture: "Do not let this book of the law depart from your
mouth; meditate on it day and night, so that you may be careful
to do everything written in it. Then you will be prosperous and
successful" (Joshua 1:8). In order for Joshua to do everything
written in the law, he had to meditate on it day and night! He had
to give complete devotion to planting the law of God in his life.
Joshua knew that there was no greater success than developing a
friendship with God.

If we consistently plant the seeds of meditation in our lives,
we will reap an abundant harvest. Here are several benefits we
receive when we meditate on scripture:

- sinks the Word more deeply into our memory
- provides better understanding of Scripture so we can
  draw out deeper truths
- reveals spiritual principles relating to Bible knowledge
- offers the surest way of meeting with God in sweet
  fellowship
- brings fresh ideas about the Word and how to please God

Let's not be like the people of Israel who repeatedly forgot
about God and the importance of retaining and living out his
Word. Hosea said of the Israelites, "I wrote for them the many
things of my law, but they regarded them as something alien"
(Hosea 8:12).

One of the greatest benefits of hiding Scripture in our hearts is that it will be there when we need it most. Let's be like Jeremiah, who said, "When your words came, I ate them, they were my joy and my heart's delight" (Jeremiah 15:16). God told the people of Israel to "fix my words in your heart and mind" (Deuteronomy 15:8). As we fix Scripture in our lives through meditation, our walk with God will become even more delightful.

Some scientists speculate that humans have up to 70,000 thoughts a day and up to forty-eight every minute.[2] Untold amount of information is floating through our brains every day. We need to stand at the door of our minds because they are constantly bombarded with images and words that are not pure, righteous, and holy. "As man thinks, so he is" (Proverbs 23:7 KJV).

This saying by Ralph Waldo Emerson has stuck with me since I first read it many years ago:

Sow a thought, reap an act.
Sow an act, reap a habit.
Sow a habit, reap a character.
Sow a character, reap a destiny.

Destiny starts with a thought. What you allow into your mind impacts your daily living. Meditation on what you've memorized allows you to ponder, reflect, capture, and hold God's thoughts throughout the day. It becomes your sword in battle against the ways of the world. The ruler of this world (Satan) wants you to give him your hope, dreams, and aspirations instead of giving them to God. If Satan can distract you so that you put your hope in such things as money, fame, popularity, and possessions, his chances of destroying your soul increases. These things are what the world uses to lure us away from God. Keep in mind what God said about the world: "Friendship with the world is hatred toward God" (James 4:4). Those are strong words! Many say they love

God, but their actions show they love the world much more. God considers this hatred toward him.

A good test to determine our depth of love for God is to look at how we spend the 86,400 seconds we have every day. Once those seconds tick away they are gone forever. How do we spend the time God has given us? Time is much more valuable than money. We can get more money, but we can't get more time. We need to give careful consideration about where we invest our most precious commodity.

God desires to have all of us—heart, mind, soul, and strength. It's easy to be captivated and mesmerized by the world; it seems to offer so much, but in the end, it's chasing after the wind. Most people in the Western world live very comfortable lives. This comfort, if we are not watchful, robs us of our longing for heaven. Paul spoke of his longing when he said, "I desire to be with Christ, which is better by far" (Philippians 1:23).

We need to use our talents for God's glory while in the tent of this body. We must often remind ourselves that this world is not our home. We should strive to be like our spiritual forefathers who longed for the world to come.

> And they admitted that they were strangers and aliens on earth. People who say such things are looking for a country of their own. If they had been thinking of the country they had left, they would have had opportunity to return, instead they were longing for a better country—a heavenly one. Therefore God is not ashamed to be called their God, for he has prepared a city for them. (Hebrews 11:13–16)

Our home is heaven, not earth (Philippians 3:20). So let's fill our lives with his Word to help us remember this spiritual truth!

If, in fact, we have roughly 70,000 thoughts running through our brains each day, what kind of thoughts are they? When I'm browsing the news on the Internet, I often come across articles that send shivers up my spine. This world is truly evil. I have a hard enough time focusing on being righteous; I don't need to be pumping evil thoughts into my mind. When I read negative articles, it has an impact my thoughts, which affects my day. Perhaps thoughts influence how we live. They create images in our minds. They lead us down a path of planting either good seed or bad, and the seed eventually blossoms into action, the fruits of which will be either good or bad, respectively. I skim news titles and do my best to avoid reading negative articles. I don't need those horrible thoughts floating around in my brain.

Paul commanded the people of Philippi to focus on good thoughts. He understood how thoughts impact our lives. He wrote, "Finally, brothers, whatever is true, whatever is noble, whatever is right, whatever pure, whatever is lovely, whatever is admirable, if anything is excellent or praiseworthy think about such things" (Philippians 4:8). He told the Corinthians, "Take captive every thought and make it obedient to Christ" (2 Corinthians 10:5). The first-century Christians didn't have nearly the amount of input coming from so many different sources as we do—TV, radio, computer games, smart devices, and so much more. Yet, Paul encouraged them to always stand guard at the door way of their mind, careful about the kind of thoughts they allowed to enter. We too need to guard the door way of our minds! All day and night we are constantly bombarded with impurity, wickedness and evil. We are frequently accosted by information that tells our minds to treat evil as good and good as evil. Isaiah, the great prophet, says, "Woe to those who call evil good and good evil, who put darkness for light and light for darkness, who put bitter for sweet and sweet for bitter" (Isaiah 5:20). We need to fight daily to protect our minds. We need to fight daily to remember what our commitment was when decided to follow Jesus. We made a firm decision that his Word would be our guide until our dying breath! It is our standard to teach us right from wrong. As our eyes are the windows to our souls, our thoughts are the windows to our actions. Let's protect our thoughts by holding firmly to the Word of God.

This world is constantly trying to steal our faith; it does this a drip at a time. Little by little, our faith is drained, and before we know it, we're tempted to go back to the vomit. Remember what Solomon said in Song of Songs: "It's the little foxes that ruin the vineyard" (2:15). The small, seemingly meaningless spiritual basics we neglect every day build on one another, having a huge impact on our faith.

The battle against worldly ways and thoughts can feel overwhelming. The Bible says, "For our struggle is not against flesh and blood, but against the spiritual forces of evil in the heavenly realms" (Ephesians 6:12). We are constantly being hounded by wolves in sheep's clothing. The way to greater discernment and wisdom in the daily battle is to consciously submit our thoughts to Jesus, to meditate on truth. If we do, the battle of overcoming the ways of this world becomes easier and less confusing. Meditation on Scripture is an excellent and effective weapon to use against Satan and his demons.

The good news about this war we wage every day is that we have spiritual weapons that can demolish evil strongholds. We have the same sword Jesus wielded against Satan in the desert. He didn't fight against Satan with the philosophical thoughts of the day. He didn't try to outwit him by positive affirmations. He fought and won the battle against this powerful foe by preaching the Word: "Take the sword of the Spirit, which is the word of God" (Ephesians 6:12).

Let's not think we're more powerful than Jesus as we battle against the world (Satan). We need to arm ourselves with the sword of his Word to be victorious in this war. We need to imitate Jesus by using the same weapon he did when Satan tempted him. We will not be able to outwit Satan and his schemes by worldly wisdom and logic. We must wield the sword of the Word of God to overcome him.

Mediation can be tedious and repetitive—that's the nature of the discipline. But remember, repetition is the mother of skill. To develop any kind of skill requires training, practice, attention, energy, and perseverance. "No discipline seems pleasant at the time, but painful. Later on, however, it produces a harvest of righteousness and peace for those who have been trained by it" (Hebrews 12:11). We must work hard to etch his Word on the fertile soil of our hearts. The result will be an abundant harvest of peace and joy that passes understanding.

Some Christians can memorize numerous songs with seeming ease, but when memorizing Scripture, they suddenly believe they don't have the brain capacity. "It's too hard to memorize and meditate. I can't stay focused." God paid a huge price so that we can have Scripture accessible any time we want. Jesus told the disciples, "Others have done the hard work, and you have reaped the benefits of their labor" (John 4:38). The apostles, prophets, and scribes throughout the ages sacrificed their lives to ensure the integrity of Scripture. And yet too many people yawn at God's Word. We may say we have no time for it. Okay, we may not say those exact words but our actions do. We'd rather read the newspaper, the latest fashion magazine or catch up on the latest world events, rather than store God's thoughts within us.

Imagine a disciple of Christ from the first century being transported to the present. I wonder if he would stare at us in bewilderment and wonder how we could neglect the Bible sitting on our desks. I'm sure he'd shake his head and say, "If you only knew what it cost us just to glimpse at Matthew's gospel!" He would probably be astounded that we'd give our time to things that aren't getting us closer to God and instead neglect the book that is filled with heavenly treasure. Let's honor our early church family by reading, studying, memorizing, and meditating on God's Word.

Chapter 5
Walk with No Excuses

*P*salm 119 is the longest chapter in the Bible. Most verses center on loving the Word of God. We aren't sure who wrote it, but the author gives us a glimpse into his love for God's Word. According to the writer, life is nothing if not lived according to Scripture. His focus was on loving, cherishing, admiring, honoring, and obeying God.

A few passages from the chapter mention how awesome God's Word is:

- Oh how I love your law! I meditate on it all day long (v. 97)
- This has been my practice: I obey your precepts (v. 56)
- How sweet are your words to my taste? Sweeter than honey to my mouth (v. 13)

This psalm shows us the incredible value of Scripture and why we should desire it more than anything. Notice how the psalmist mentioned what it took to burn Scripture into his daily living: "This has been my practice" (v. 56). Memorizing takes consistent, daily practice and focus; discipline and hard work. It's not a walk in the park, but if you embark on this journey, your life will never be the same.

You might be thinking, *I can't memorize a single passage never mind a whole book or several books!* Or maybe you feel overwhelmed just at the mention of memorizing Scripture. Perhaps you're thinking, *there's no way I can memorize more than "For God so loved the world that he gave his one and only son."* You can probably quote book, chapter, and verse of this selection because you've seen it, read it, and heard it many times before. And this proves the point that memorizing—any length of passage— is possible through repetition. God can do more than we ask or imagine. I believe that 99 percent of believers have the ability but lack desire.

Let me share the most common excuses I've heard for not memorizing God's Word:

1. **No time.** We manage to find time for whatever we desire to do most. It's a matter of setting priorities. Everyone has twenty-four hours in a day. How are you spending those hours? Are you too busy to do what is important for God and your relationship with him? Remember, you'll take into heaven what you've put into practice here. Your walk with him should be of first importance.

2. **Pressure of earning a living/going to school.** Cares of this life always seem to assert themselves against our spiritual pursuits. It's easy in our fast-moving world to feast the body and famish the soul. If you lose your desire for the Word, spiritual lethargy will set in.

3. **I don't have a good memory.** "I'm too old." "I'm too young." "I already have too much work to do." Remember, almost anyone can memorize God's Word. It's not lack of talent but a lack of desire that stops us. Ask God for help. "I can do everything through him who gives me strength" (Philippians 4:13). If you don't use it, you'll lose it. But if you use it, you'll strengthen it. There is no rush in memorizing. Just do it. Your ability to memorize will improve. If you don't use a muscle, it

will atrophy; if you exercise it, it will strengthen. This is also true for your brain.

4. **Feeling disappointed by not being able to recall all memorized verses.** It's easy to get disappointed and discouraged, but prepare yourself for this eventuality. Everything takes practice, practice, practice before it becomes a skill. Understand that the only way anybody can recall memorized scriptures for any length of time is by constant use of these verses. Reciting them out loud to yourself or a loved one will help to seal the words on your heart.

5. **Why bother memorizing Scripture when I have a Bible a click away on my smartphone?** Remember that memorizing is much more than having access to information or gaining knowledge. It's a beautiful, intimate process for us to bond with God. When we spend time with him, he is spending time us (2 Chronicles 15:2). As we repeat this practice as often as possible, a deeper relationship is formed. His Word living in us gives us the strength to resist conforming to the pattern of this world. It's a continual reminder to help us keep important what is important.

I have moments when my memory fails me, such as when I meet someone and forget his or her name in a matter of seconds. The problem isn't my memory; it's my focus. If I repeat this person's name often enough, I'll never forget it.

I was almost voted Most Absentminded my senior year in high school. *Almost.* (My wife is convinced that award was mine) As a child and throughout my teen years, I never willingly read a book on my own. It was hard for me to retain knowledge when reading books or attending classes. I was way down in rank in my class of 250. I didn't lack intelligence. I lacked desire. I didn't care about learning. I was into sports, friends, partying, and dating. Nothing else mattered.

I became a disciple when I was twenty, and God changed me. I bought my first book, *The Greatest Salesman in the World*. From that point on, my love for books intensified. I became a voracious reader. I wanted to learn as much as I could about anything and everything. After I became a disciple, I focused on being a great student. I graduated with a double major and a GPA of 3.6. A far cry from the 1.0 I earned my freshman year. Everyone can develop and nurture the qualities of discipline and determination to memorize large sections of scripture (1 Timothy 1:7). Everyone can and should be a good student of God's Word.

Lately, I seem to be thinking about a list of things I need to do and then a few seconds later, I forget what's on the list. Can you relate? I wish I had a photographic memory, but it's just a wish. It's taken a lot of practice and many years of hard work to memorize scripture, but no one is ever too old to develop memory muscle. When we get older, our brains may shrink and harden from lack of use. However, the best therapy for the brain is exercise and one of the best exercises is memorization. And nothing is healthier for the brain of a disciple than memorizing Scripture. I'm living testimony. I stand in awe of how God has moved me to memorize so many passages of Scripture. This maxim is true: We put forth the effort, and God blesses the results.

We should be like the psalmist who said, "Blessed is the man [and woman] who delights in the law of the Lord, and on his law he meditates day and night" (Psalm 1:2). You can memorize whatever you set your mind to. As the cliché says, if you believe, you will achieve. What are some things you can recall from memory? Maybe a bunch of phone numbers, lyrics to a song, sports stats? What about the Lord's Prayer, the Pledge of Allegiance, The Star-Spangled Banner? We memorize what's important, and it sticks with us as we repeat it.

How important is Scripture to you?

As Josh McDowell says in *The Evidence that Demands a Verdict*,

> The Bible has withstood vicious attacks by its enemies. Many have tried to burn it, ban it, and outlaw it from the days of Roman emperors to present-day Communist-dominated countries. In A.D. 303, the Roman emperor Diocletian issued an edict to stop Christians from worshiping and to destroy their Scriptures.[1]

He failed. Praise Jesus!

Again, we don't lack capacity or potential—we lack desire, discipline, and focus. A story is written in Bart Bagget's *Success Secrets* about a neurological study done on an ape. The scientists taped down all except one of the ape's fingers and had the ape move its one un-taped finger up and down repeatedly. When they removed the tape from his fingers, the one finger was still moving up and down. As the neuroscientist observed the ape's brain, he noted neuropathways being developed through the repeated movement.[2]

The same happens when we continuously go over Scripture. The repetition eventually burns the words of God into our neuropathways. "It turns out that we, as human beings, develop neural pathways, and the more we use those neural pathways over years and years and years, they become very stuck and deeply embedded, moving into deeper portions of the brain," wrote Deborah Ancona, a professor of management and organizational studies at MIT.[3] The more you repeat the verses you love, the better the chance they will remain in you. You can have his words carved into your brain, ready to be used at a moment's notice. All that is required is discipline, practice, and *reasons*.

When the why is important and big enough, the how is easy. This is true no matter what we set out to achieve. If we don't have enough reasons to do something, we give up. And if the goal is really big, we need really big reasons to do it!

I recently finished an Ironman triathlon in Louisville, Kentucky. It required a year of training, and the last six months demanded over twenty hours a week on the bike, in the pool, and on the road running—two workouts a day. Granted, my body was already acclimated to embrace the training because I had done many half- and full-distance events prior to this. As you can imagine, the rigorous training is taxing on the mind and body. You can't just show up the day of the event and say, "I'm ready. I've done a few 10-k races." To complete an event like an Ironman, a training program is a must-do. You keep missed days at a minimum, unless you want to suffer more than you should.

The distance of an Ironman is 140.6 miles: a 2.4 mile swim, a 112-mile bike ride, and a 26.2-mile run. I had to come up with some big reasons why I wanted to put my body (and my family) through such a long and arduous training program again. Without reasons, it would have become much easier to quit once the challenges piled up.

The *journey* to the starting line of an IM event is much tougher than the event itself. It took me eleven hours and thirty minutes to finish. I had many reasons why I wanted to finish this triathlon, the main reason was to prove to myself that I was physically and mentally capable of completing this event at age forty-nine. No matter how much suffering I had to endure (and I did indeed suffer!), I was determined to complete my goal.

If you want to accomplish any challenging goal, you must have big reasons.

If you desire to memorize Scripture, you need reasons why you want to embark on this journey. And if you want to memorize large sections of the Bible, the reasons must be bigger. A good idea to keep in mind is to prayerfully consider the reasons why you want to memorize. You should then write your thoughts in a journal. If you are ever tempted to quit, you can review the reasons why you embarked on this journey to begin with. This plan will help keep you focused, and the excuses tend to flee.

Prior to memorizing books of the Bible, I knew a few verses. When I was a young Christian, I didn't have many reasons to believe that memorization would impact me. As I began this journey of writing his Word on my heart, my desire to know God began to increase.

The early days of memorization are the hardest. The gospel of John contains 15,635 words in twenty-one chapters. When I started thinking about memorizing it, the mental battle began: *You want to memorize all those chapters? It's one thing to memorize 2 Timothy, but John? Don't you know who you are? You have a poor memory, and you have a tough time remembering anything for a long time.* I continuously wrestled with doubt as I embarked on the journey to capture the words of John on my heart.

Fast-forward twenty-three years. If you were to ask me to recite the whole book of John, I could. That's because I had big reasons—I wanted to know Jesus more deeply. I wanted to make him and the Father proud. I wanted to become better friends with them. I wanted my respect, fear and admiration of them to grow. I have a long way to go, but having John consistently on my mind has helped me to better know them over the years.

During the early days of my quest to memorize, it felt like it was never going to get easier. However, over time, the more verses and chapters I memorized, the easier it became. Honestly, I had frustrating moments, but I stuck with it. Now I have the joy of reciting many passages during my time with Jesus.

Memorizing is the best therapy for improving memory. Nothing replaces repetition.

Memorization happens by being relentless in your focus. Maybe you need to enjoy the fruits of smaller victories. Perhaps start memorizing 2 John—thirteen verses but rich in meaning. Maybe take a chapter from a gospel you really like. Whatever your plan, make sure you devise big reasons why it's important to accomplish this goal. When you feel like you're losing hope, review your reasons for memorizing or you are welcome to email me at **writtenonyourheart@hotmail.com** or visit the website **www.writtenonyourheart.com**. I'll do my best to encourage you to keep on keeping on. If you are feeling frustrated one day, leave it for the next. Remember, God gave us memory "so we could have roses in December." Bury your excuses about why something can't be done. He gave each of us a beautiful mind.

As noted in the bookboon blog, the famed psychologist Norman Cousins says, "Not even the universe with all its countless billions of galaxies represents greater wonder or complexity than the human brain." The blog also mentions, "Your brain has enough atomic energy to build any of the world's major cities many times over. Unsurprisingly, no human being has yet existed who has been able to use all the potential of the brain."[4] And there have been some very smart people.

When I started out memorizing 2 Timothy, my main motivation was to meet the requirement of the class. I had small thinking. I put limits around my brain. However, as I repeatedly pondered Paul's words to Timothy, their love for each other inspired me. Also, Paul's vision for young Timothy's future encouraged me. That letter taught me to believe the best of others.

One of the greatest blessings of being disciples is knowing our friendships with those in God's church can be centered on honesty, openness, vulnerability, and acceptance. This book taught me those lessons and more. The inspiration didn't happen right away, but, over time, my heart fell in love with the message in 2 Timothy, which contains many great lessons. As those lessons moved me to maturity and growth, I wanted to write more of his Word on my heart. Some of my favorite passages found in this book are, "For God did not give us a spirit of timidity, but a spirit of power, of love, and of self-discipline" (1:7) and "I have fought the good fight. I have finished the race. I have kept the faith" (4:7).

A walk with God is a marathon, not a sprint. Depending on when you become a Christian and how long you live, your Christian race is more like an Ultraman (ten Ironman races). It's like repeatedly fighting Mike Tyson in his prime. It is hard work living a pure and holy life in a world saturated with evil. What is the award we receive for fighting the fight of faith and winning? Paul wrote that it is a crown of righteousness the Lord will give to all who cross the finish line (2 Timothy 4:8). We run this race not to get a crown that withers but a crown that lasts for eternity (1 Corinthians 9:25).

I began memorizing Timothy because it was expected of me. However, over time, the words moved me into having a much deeper appreciation for this amazing book. My reasons evolved from being a requirement to hungering for God.

Once I saw how much I grew from having written 2 Timothy on my heart, I wanted to memorize more. My next goal was to memorize Philippians. That book has given me much joy in life. It has helped me better understand that no matter how difficult life may become, I can rejoice in the Lord always. I can have a peace that passes understanding when chaos is happening all around me. Paul was in prison suffering, and he wrote this letter of encouragement. What excuse do I have for not being joyful?

The following verses have been a constant source of encouragement for me over the years:

- Rejoice in the Lord always. I will say it again, rejoice (4:4)
- Your attitude should be the same as that of Christ Jesus (2:7)
- Do everything without complaining or arguing (2:14)
- I want to know Christ (3:10)
- But one thing I do, forgetting what is behind, and straining on towards what is ahead (3:13)

Many verses in this book make me smile every time I recite them.

Once I memorized 2 Timothy as well as Philippians, my confidence increased and my reasons continued to multiply. The next book I focused on was Colossians. In a relatively short time, I memorized three books Paul had written from prison. He inspired me with his faith-filled passion to glorify God no matter the circumstances. What I thought was impossible when I began this journey was morphing into an increased hunger and thirst for his Word.

After those three books came the huge goal of memorizing John's gospel. I had to clear my mind of all excuses and come up with some mighty big reasons why I wanted to accomplish this goal. I've spent a lot of years pondering, wrestling, crying out, praying over, and meditating on this most amazing book. Even after all these years of reciting this gospel, it continues to deepen my understanding of Jesus as nothing else does.

One of my goals at the end of 2016 was to recite the twenty-one chapters of John each day for seven days. After three days, I began thinking more deeply about Jesus and his relationship with the Father. A blend of verses began to flood my mind about the special relationship they shared, and I was gaining a deeper appreciation for it. The pages of John are filled with many passages in which Jesus talks about his Father (134 times). I never really got to know my dad. Besides, what does a young kid know about getting to know his father better? I had no clue. Especially considering mine was deaf. But these verses moved me to start thinking about the dad I had lost to cancer when I was fourteen. He was beset by physical and mental illness a few years before his passing.

With what I know now, if I could turn back the clock of time, I would have made more of an effort to spend time with my dad and ask him lots of questions. I remember the day of his passing thirty-five years ago as if it were yesterday. I was a freshman in high school playing basketball in the gym with some friends. A voice came over the loudspeaker: "Michael Arsenault [my older brother] and Bobby Arsenault, please report to the front office." I met my brother and his track coach there, and he drove us home. The home where we lived was a 3rd floor attic converted into an apartment. It was a tiny place. This is where my dad lay sick.

When we got home, I ran upstairs as fast as I could. My heart was pounding. A nurse with tears in her eyes met me at the door. She looked at me with compassion and said, "Oh, Bobby. Oh, Bobby."

I moved past her and ran into the room where my father lay motionless. My knees buckled. My head went into his stomach. I wept uncontrollably. As a fourteen-year-old, I knew little about life, but I knew that moment would forever change me. As the tears streamed down my face, a few people gathered around the bed. I looked up and said, "Uncle David, please, please wake him up. Please give me a chance to say I love you and good-bye one last time. Please." All he could do was bow his head in silence. That chance would never come. That sad day is forever etched upon my soul. He was only forty-nine when he passed. I never got the chance to know my father.

As for Jesus, he never knew what life was like without a dad. They were inseparable. They had been together forever: "And now Father, glorify me in your presence with the glory I had with you before the world began" (John 17:5). They were completely and thoroughly satisfied in their love for one another. We have little information about what life was like for them before Jesus wrapped himself with flesh and entered time and space. We know countless angels were singing their praise. We have to imagine that heaven is a gazillion times better than anything this world has to offer. Our feeble minds, even with our wild imaginations, can't imagine what it's like.

When Jesus entered the world his Father was by his side. They were still very intimate with each other, but their relationship was a bit different when Jesus was on earth. To our knowledge, it wasn't as if the Father revealed his full glory when spending time with Jesus on earth. Jesus had to walk with God the same way we do: trust, faith, and obedience. Jesus became aware of the uniqueness of his relationship with his Father when he was at least twelve, maybe sooner; Scripture doesn't say. When Joseph and Mary found Jesus at the temple after three days of searching for him, they asked, "Didn't you know we've been anxiously searching everywhere for you?" (Luke 2:48). Jesus replied, "Didn't you know I had to be in my Father's house?" (v. 49). And he was only twelve! We see the details of this intimate relationship blossom in the gospel of John. Let's look at a few of the many passages in John that describe the beauty of this amazing relationship between Jesus and the Father.

> When Phillip asked Jesus to show him the Father, Jesus said, "Don't you know me Phillip even after I've been among you for such a long time? Anyone who has seen me, has seen the Father. How can you say show us the Father? Don't you believe that I am in the Father and that the Father is in me? The words I say to you are not just my own, rather it is the Father living in me doing his work. Believe me when I say that I am in the father and the Father is in me" (14:9–11).

> "When he looks at me, he sees the one who sent me" (John 12:45).

> "Believe the miracles that you may know and understand that the Father is in me, and I in the Father" (10:37).

The picture of the Son and the Father is beautiful. Scripture teaches that Jesus often went off by himself to talk with the Father: "Very early in the morning, while it was still dark, Jesus got up, left the house and went off to a solitary place, where he prayed" (Mark 1:35). His reliance on the Father while in the flesh is inspiring (See chapter 16). As we noted above, everything Jesus did, everything he said, was from the Father. It's very difficult for me to grasp just how close their relationship was during his sojourn on earth, but I liken it to the many laughs and fun I have while building wonderful memories with my family.

Jesus knew his Father would be with him always, to comfort him even when his best friends deserted him: "You will leave me all lone, yet I'm not alone, for my Father is with me" (John 16:32). The Father was with his Son during the most physically intense moments Jesus endured—the scourging, the thorns jammed into his skull, the rods slamming against his head, the punches from the guards, and the nails ripping through his hands and feet. The Father was by his Son's side through it all. The cross was designed to cause the maximum pain for the longest time, a tortuous death for criminals. The Father was with the Son as he suffered. He was with the Son as his heart broke seeing his mother weep at his feet while hanging on this tool of torment. The Father would never leave the Son, until . . .

There came a moment when Jesus experienced the horror of his Father's absence from his side. It was a pain so deep and hurtful that I don't believe even the physical suffering he endured compared with it. Yes, Jesus knew in advance he would endure incredible pain (John 18:4). The anxiety of his suffering was so real that while praying to the Father in the olive grove, the sweat on his forehead looked like blood (Luke 22:44). I'm certain that the stress of realizing he would have to sustain extreme suffering was part of the reason why this occurred. But perhaps he was also coming to the frightening comprehension that for the first time ever, his Father would abandon him! The Father and Son had never known separation until that fateful moment on the cross.

While hanging on the cross, Jesus sensed something was seriously wrong. He felt a shocking emptiness inside. The Father, *who had lived in him* during his days on earth, was no longer present. The One who had been with his Son from eternity decided it was time to forsake him. I can't imagine the heartache the Father must have felt to leave Jesus in this condition. I think of my children not being able to find me if lost and it moves me to tears. But to see them lost or being hurt and then knowing I could do something about it but don't—that would crush me. This tore at the Father's heart.

Jesus sensed this void inside and knew the Father would not return to comfort him; he cried out, *"Eloi, Eloi, lama sabachthani?"*—"My God, My God, why have you forsaken me?" (Matthew 27:45). Vocabulary.com gives an insightful definition into the word *forsaken*: "It suggests leaving someone behind when they need you the most." When Jesus was in desperate need of his Father's presence, he was nowhere to be found. He had left his Son behind to contend with the full brunt of our sin. He who had no sin took on our sin (2 Corinthians 5:21).

I have to imagine all of heaven was silent at that moment. Why had the Father abandoned his Son? Because of my selfishness, greed, idolatry, impurity, pride, hate, and many other sins. The Father and Son were separated for the first time ever because of my sin—your sin! It had to happen or we would never know the blessing of eternal life or the blessing of getting to know the Father and Son intimately during our life on earth (See chapter 11).

These were some of the thoughts that flooded my mind as I recited the twenty-one chapters of John over those seven days. It gave me a profound sense of gratitude for the incredible gift of salvation. If I hadn't buried the excuses to memorize this beautiful book, I may have never gained these insights into the majestic love between Father and son.

Though I lost my earthly father when I was young, God the Father stepped in and has taken care of me ever since I made my commitment at age nineteen to follow Jesus. I haven't been a saint. I've been unfaithful to God many times over the last thirty years. However, he has remained faithful. Second Timothy 2:13 says it well: "If we are faithless, he will remain faithful, for he cannot disown himself." The Father loved us so much that he forsook his Son. Jesus loved us so much that he allowed it to happen. Thank God!

Chapter 6
Walk with Focus

*I*t doesn't matter how long it takes you to memorize. Don't rush it. Relax and relish the sweetness of the Word as you joyfully chisel it on your heart. Consider each word, each phrase, and each sentence. Say it out loud to yourself or to others. Say it with expression and conviction. Use your imagination. Involve as many senses as possible. Envision the scenario being portrayed.

Memorization boils down to concentration and repetition. You have to block everything out of your mind and set your full attention on the Word. Satan knows you'll defeat his power in your life in proportion to the way you allow the Word of Christ to dwell in you richly.

If I were to ask 1,000 faithful Christians if memorization was important, I'd be willing to bet all of them would agree. But how many put it into practice? Unfortunately, I would guess not many. Many Christians don't have a desire to memorize because they don't have any reasons to do so. Perhaps they're not interested because of what it requires to be successful: determination, discipline, concentration, and energy—daily.

Remember what Paul said to Timothy: "God did not give us a spirit of timidity, but a spirit of love, power and self-discipline" (2 Timothy 1:7). God gave us a spirit of self-discipline, and we have the ability to act with discipline. The question is, will we?

Recall from the previous chapter the most common excuses for not memorizing God's Word. Can you relate? What are some of the obstacles you wrestle with in your quest to memorize?

- No time
- Pressure of earning a living/going to school
- I don't have a good memory
- Feeling disappointed not being able recall all memorized verses
- Why bother memorizing Scripture when I have a Bible a click away on my smartphone?

Here some ideas that have helped me memorize.

Reason: As mentioned earlier, determine great reasons for memorizing Scripture. They will help motivate you. Why are you memorizing? What's your goal? Why is it important to memorize those selected passages or chapters or books of Scripture? Memorization is less about ability and more about desire, which motivates you to start memorizing your favorite selections. Do you love a particular psalm? Has a chapter helped you through a difficult time and holds a special place in your heart? That connection will help you as you learn to memorize.

Recite: Say the words out loud to someone or to an audio recorder app on your smartphone. Make sure you have it word perfect. Read it out loud several times. When you read silently, the picture is not clearly in view and your mind is apt to wander, but when you read it out loud, the picture becomes more vivid. Out-loud recitation is the most effective way to memorize. Preach to yourself. Be animated. Involve your imagination. And then repeat. Nothing beats repetition.

Recollection: Move on to a different task for a while before going back to recite the passage. Memorization is better done in short periods with lapses of time to help lock the material into your mind. Overlearn the verses—go over them again and again. Reinforce them in your brain as you did when you began to learn to ride a bike.

Retain: The goal of memorizing is to retain Scripture for the rest of your life. There are lots of reasons to retain the verses you have determined to memorize. It can help us in all situations. It helps us to live life to the full. It motivates us to remain close to God

A Few Instructions

Persevere. You must want it. Desire is half the battle of accomplishing the task. He can do immeasurably more than we can ask or imagine. Be positive and faith filled. You can do it!

Overview. Use commentaries and other helpful aids to assist you in better understanding what you are memorizing. Try to make the passages real to you. How do they impact you? What insights do you glean about Jesus's character? What is the meaning of what you're learning? Answers to these questions may better equip you when faced with challenges or discouragement.

Read Out Loud. Read the verses out loud several times. Go over them again and again. I use my ten fingers for verses—verse one is my thumb, verse five is my pinky, six is my other thumb, and ten is my other pinky. I use this system to cover chapters and books. Eventually, I don't need my fingers to remember. Please visit the website

writtenonyourheart.com to find some helpful aids to assist you in your quest to memorize.

Go over the verses as much as you can throughout the day and before you go to bed. When you know a chapter verbatim, begin this process on the next chapter. Every day go over the chapter you've memorized before working on the new one. Again, this isn't easy but you're storing up treasures that will last an eternity.

Memorize Continually. Once you complete a group of verses or a chapter, continue to go over them as often as possible. You must be consistent in your approach. Maybe your "normal" quiet time takes a backseat for several months, or maybe it is shortened. Give yourself a lot of time to memorize a big chunk of Scripture. You must repeat often. Repetition is the mother of skill.

Continuous Reminders. You can write the verses out on cards and carry them with you at all times. I know I'm about to commit heresy in some people's view, but I used to rip pages out of a Bible and use them as my memory aid. When I started on the gospel of John, I put the pages of the Bible on my steering wheel—a big no-no. That was back in 1994, before we were warned against texting while driving. I had a 4 hour drive to work every day (2 hours up and back). It was during this time I memorized John. I don't recommend this today. If you have a long commute, discover safer methods to help you memorize while you're in the car.

Use Your Senses. Say the words out loud. Write them out. Imagine the scenario being played out. Pray over the words as you learn them. Talk with others about them. Pretend you're in front of an audience. Share the words as though you were speaking with them. I see the words on the page in my mind after a while. Your learning style might be different, so use what works best for you.

But remember: nothing replaces repetition. When you believe you have the selection down pat, share them with someone else. It's when you're looking someone in the eyes while reciting that puts your memorization skills to the test.

Review. You have more free time than you realize. Even when you have a few spare moments, use that time to review what you've memorized that day. Again, give yourself *six to twelve months* to memorize a book of the Bible. Commit to this practice. Follow through every day on the plan you develop. Remember the reasons why you're memorizing scripture. Keep a Bible with you or index cards you've written verses on. As I mentioned earlier, I used pages torn from my Bible as my index cards. Oh, and make sure you stick with the same translation. Mine is the NIV 1984 version.

Schedule Time. Carve out a specific time of the day to recite Scripture. Make sure you have a place where you aren't distracted. These days, it's hard to get away from all distractions because it seems computers and gadgets follow us everywhere. But you must find a way to quiet your mind and soul so you can have focused time on memorizing out loud God's Word. "If anyone is thirsty let him come to me and drink" (John 7:37). Let Jesus satisfy your deepest longing.

PART TWO

Sweeter Than Honey

Chapters seven through sixteen are a high level overview of several important subjects found in Scripture. These basic studies are meant for everyone. My prayer is that if you don't know Jesus as your Lord and Savior, these subjects will help you begin your quest of becoming a Christian. If you are a believer, I pray that they serve as reminders of what is essential for all Christians, no matter how long you've been a disciple.

The studies in the following chapters are designed as a general overview to encourage you to dig deeper into these topics. As you go through them, you will find a plethora of verses; perhaps you can add additional passages to the list (additional notes section).

We often need to be reminded about what is important. I know I do! The apostle Peter clearly pointed out our need to hear truth repeated again and again:

> "*So I will <u>always remind you</u> of these things,* even though you know them and are firmly established in the truth you now have. I think it right to refresh your memory as long as I live in the tent of this body, because I know that I will put it aside,

as our Lord Jesus Christ has made clear to me. And I will make every effort to see that after my departure *you will always be able to remember these things*. . . . Dear Friends, this is now my second letter to you. *I have written both of them as reminders* to stimulate you to whole thinking." (2 Peter 1:12–15; 3:1–2, emphasis mine)

Even though Peter was writing to Christians who knew "these things," he frequently urged them to always hold firmly to the basic teachings of God. They are the foundation blocks from which we build an eternal relationship with Jesus. As disciples, we must have a firm understanding and belief that *all Scripture* is from God.

Chapter seven contains an overview of why we need to make the Bible the standard for how we live. The more we read it, *and put it into practice*, the more our faith will grow. It is God's promise. His words are living and active and are applicable to our lives today, tomorrow, and forevermore!

Next, as his disciples we must have a strong faith about who Jesus is. In chapters eight and nine, I share passages describing the deity and humanity of Jesus. He was not only God, he was also fully human. Not only did Jesus claim to be God, but his best friends affirmed it. If anyone could point out flaws in Jesus's life, it was those who spent every waking moment with him for three years. They saw every nuance of his character, and yet they claimed he was without sin and, in fact, was God. It's one thing to die for a lie not knowing it was a lie; however, it's doubtful that anyone would die for a lie *knowing it is a lie*. Most of the apostles died horrific deaths because of their faith that Jesus was God in the flesh.

In chapter ten we discuss that "forbidden word": *sin*. God takes our sin very seriously, and we discuss why in chapter eleven. We, too, should not treat it lightly.

In chapter twelve I share some passages about the importance of being a new creation, and at what point this transformation happens.

In chapter thirteen, we look at what it means to be a disciple of Jesus. The New Testament frequently mentions the words *disciple*, *student*, and *follower*. We should have a fundamental understanding of what it means to be a disciple of Jesus *before* we make a lifelong commitment to walk in his steps.

Chapter fourteen highlights several reasons why it is important to build best friendships with other disciples. The church is not a building to go to but a group of people we look forward to being with.

Chapter fifteen is a reminder about how God loves each of us individually. Let's take great comfort in knowing he has hand selected each one of us to love and adore. Let's reciprocate that love!

Next is a study on the prayer life of Jesus. If he relied on the Father, so should we! We also look at other passages that should inspire us to pray more.

In chapter seventeen I share some Psalms that I've written on my heart to better equip me to adore and praise Jesus. Memorizing Psalms can help us be more effective at praising God.

Last, I share some fun facts about the power of our brain.

Chapter 7
Living and Active

For us to gain greater faith about things spiritual we must read, search, study, meditate, and apply Scripture to our lives. Paul wrote that faith comes from hearing the message and the message is heard through the Word of Christ (Romans 10:17). If you want to learn about who Jesus is, what your purpose in life is, where you came from, how much God loves you and why, and much more, you need to read God's Word. If we have little faith, I suspect we have been in God's Word very little. Dig deep into the Bible, for in it God gives us everything we need for life and godliness (2 Peter 1:3). Be diligent to put Scripture to use. As the saying goes, use it or lose it. I'd like to alter that just a bit to: use it, or lose it, and then be deceived. "Do not merely listen to the word, and so deceive yourselves. Do what it says" (James 1:22). Below are scriptures that remind us of the power of God's Word.

> Matthew 24:35: "Heaven and earth will pass away, but my words will never pass away."
>
> Matthew 7:24: "Therefore everyone who hears these words of mine and puts them into practice is like a wise man who built his house on the rock."
>
> Matthew 4:4: "'Jesus answered, 'It is written: "Man shall not live on bread alone, but on every word that comes from the mouth of God.'"

Luke 11:28: "He replied, 'Blessed rather are those who hear the word of God and obey it.'"

2 Timothy 3:16: "All scripture is God breathed and is useful for teaching, correcting, rebuking and training in righteousness, so that the man of God may be thoroughly equipped for every good work."

2 Peter 2:21: "Above all, you must understand that no prophecy of Scripture came about by the prophet's own interpretation. For prophecy never had its origin in the will of man, but men spoke from God as they were carried along by the Holy Spirit."

James 1:22: "Do not merely listen to the word, and so deceive yourselves. Do what it says. Anyone who listens to the word but does not do what it says is like a man who looks at his face in a mirror and, after looking at himself, goes away and immediately forget what he looks like. But the man who looks intently into the perfect law that gives freedom, and continues to this, not forgetting what he has heard, but doing it—he will be blessed in what he does."

Hebrews 2:1: "We must pay more careful attention, therefore to what we have heard, so that we do not drift away."

Hebrews 1:3: "The Son is the radiance of God's glory and the exact representation of his being, sustaining all things by his powerful word."

Hebrews 4:12: "For the word of God is living and active. Sharper than any double-edged sword, it penetrates even to dividing soul and spirit, joins and marrow; it judges the thoughts and attitudes of the heart."

2 Timothy 2:14: "Do your best to present yourself to God as one approved, a workman who does not need to be ashamed and who correctly handles the word of truth."

2 Timothy 3:14: "But as for you, continue in what you have learned and have convinced of, because you know those from whom you learned it, and how from infancy you

have known the holy Scriptures, which are able to make you wise for salvation through faith in Christ Jesus."

2 Timothy 2:8: "Remember Jesus Christ, raised from the dead, descended from David. This is my gospel, for which I am suffering even to the point of being chained like a criminal. But God's Word is not chained."

1 Timothy 6:3: "If anyone teaches false doctrines and does not agree to the sound instruction of our Lord Jesus Christ and to godly teaching, he is conceited and understand nothing."

2 Thessalonians 3:1: "Finally, brothers, pray for us that the message of the Lord may spread rapidly and be honored, just as it was with you."

2 Thessalonians 2:8: "He will punish those who do not know God and do not obey the gospel of our Lord Jesus."

2 Thessalonians 4:18: "Therefore encourage each other with these words."

2 Thessalonians 4:8: "Therefore, he who rejects this instruction does not reject man but God, who gives you his Holy Spirit."

2 Thessalonians 2:13: "And we also thank God continually because, when you received the word of God, which you heard from us, you accepted it not as the word of men, but as it actually is, the word of God, which is at work in you who believe."

2 Thessalonians 2:8: "We loved you so much that we were delighted to share with you not only the gospel of God but our lives as well, because you had become so dear to us."

Colossians 3:16: "**Let the word of Christ dwell in you richly** as you teach and admonish one another with all wisdom, and as you sing psalms, hymns, and spiritual songs with gratitude in your hearts to God" (emphasis mine).

Ephesians 6:13; 17: "Therefore put on the full armor of God, so that when the day of evil comes, you be able to stand your ground, and after you have done everything, to stand. Take the helmet of salvation and the sword of the Spirit, which is the word of God."

Philippians 4:8–9: "Finally, brothers, whatever is true, whatever is noble, whatever is right, whatever is pure, whatever is lovely, whatever is admirable—if anything is excellent or praiseworthy—think about such things. Whatever you have learned or received or heard from me, or seen in me—put it into practice. And the God of peace will be with you."

Galatians 6:6: "Anyone who receives instruction in the word must share all good things with his instructor."

Galatians 1:11: "I want you to know, brothers, that the gospel I preached is not something that man made up. I did not receive it from any man, nor was I taught it rather; I received it by revelation from Jesus Christ."

Galatians 1:9: "As we have already said, so now I say again: If anybody is preaching to you a gospel other than what you accepted, let him be eternally condemned."

1 Corinthians 15:1: "Now, brothers, I want to remind you of the gospel I preached to you, which you received and which you have taken your stand. By this gospel you are saved, if you hold firmly to the word I preached to you. Otherwise, you have believed in vain."

Romans 15:4: "For everything that was written in the past was written to teach us, so that through endurance and the encouragement of the Scriptures we have hope."

Romans 10:17: "Consequently, faith comes from hearing the message, and the message is heard through the word of Christ."

Amos 8:11: "The days are coming, declares the Sovereign Lord, when I will send a famine through the land—not a famine of food or thirst for water, but a famine of hearing the word of the Lord. Men will stagger from sea to sea and wander from North to East, searching for the word of the Lord, but they will not find it."

Hosea 8:12: "I wrote for them the many things of my law, but they regarded them as something alien."

Jeremiah 31:33: "I will put my law in their minds and write it on their hearts."

Jeremiah 20:9: "But if I say, I will not mention him or speak any more in his name, his word is in my heart like a fire, a fire shut up in my bones. I am weary of holding it in; indeed, I cannot."

Isaiah 55:8: "For my thoughts are not your thoughts, neither are your ways my ways," declares the Lord. "As the heavens are higher than the earth so are my ways higher than your ways and my thoughts than your thoughts. As the rain and the snow come down from heaven and do not return to it without watering the earth and making it bud and flourish, so that it yields seed for the sower and bread for the eater, so is my word that goes out from my mouth: It will not return to me empty, but I will accomplish what I desire and achieve the purpose for which I sent it."

Isaiah 42:21: "It pleased the Lord for the sake of his righteousness to make his law great and glorious"

Isaiah 40:7: "The grass withers and the flowers fall, because the breath of the Lord blows on them. Surely the people are grass. The grass withers and the flowers fall, **but the word of the Lord stands forever**" (emphasis mine).

Proverbs 30:5: "Every word of God is flawless; he is a shield to those who take refuge in him. Do not add to his words, or he will rebuke you and prove you a liar."

Proverbs 22:17: "Pay attention and listen to the sayings of the wise; apply your heart to what I teach, for it is pleasing when you keep them in your heart and have all of them ready on your lips."

Proverbs 3:1–2: "My son, do not forget my teaching, but keep my commands in your heart, for they will prolong your life many years, and bring you prosperity."

Proverbs 2:1–5: "My son, if you accept my words and store up my commands within you, turning your ear to wisdom and applying your heart to understanding, and if you call out for insight and cry aloud for understanding, and if you look for it as for silver and search for it as hidden treasure, then you will understand the fear of the Lord and find the knowledge of God."

Psalm 130:5: "I wait for the Lord, my whole being waits, and in his word I put my hope."

Most of Psalm 119 speaks of the awesomeness of God's Word. Here are several I cherish.

Psalm 119:160: "All your words are true; all your righteous laws are eternal."

Psalm 119:140: "Your promises have been thoroughly tested, and your servant loves them."

Psalm 119:114: "You are my refuge and my shield; I have put my hope in your word."

Psalm 119:105: "Your word is a lamp for my feet, a light on my path."

Psalm 119:89: "Your word, Lord, is eternal; it stands firm in the heavens."

Psalm 119:48: "I reach out for your commands, which I love, that I may meditate on your decrees."

Psalm 119:16: "I delight in your decrees; I will not neglect your word."

Psalm 119:11: "I have hidden your word in my heart that I might not sin against you."

Psalm 119:9: "How can a young keep his way pure? By living according to your word."

Psalm 40:8: "I desire to do your will, O my God; your law is within my heart."

Psalm 37:31: "The law of his God is in his heart; his feet do not slip."

Psalm 33:4: "For the word of the Lord is right and true; he is faithful in all he does."

Psalm 33:6: "By the word of the Lord were the heavens made, their starry host by the breath of his mouth."

Psalm 19:8: "The precepts of the Lord are right, giving joy to the heart. The commands of the Lord are radiant, giving light to the eyes."

Psalm 19:9–11: "The ordnances of the Lord are sure and altogether righteous. They are more precious than gold, than much pure gold; they are sweeter than honey, than honey from the comb. By them your servant is warned; in keeping them there is great reward."

Psalm 19:7: "The law of the Lord is perfect, reviving the soul."

Psalm 18:30: "As for God, his way is perfect; the word of the Lord is flawless."

Psalm 1:2: "But his delight is in the law of the Lord, and on his law he meditates day and night."

Job 23:12: "I have not departed from the commands of his lips; I have treasured the words of his mouth more than my daily bread."

Job 21-22: "Submit to God and be at peace with him; in this way prosperity will come to you. Accept instruction from his mouth and lay up his words in your heart."

Nehemiah 8:5; 8; 18: "Ezra opened the book. All the people could see him because he was standing above them; and as he opened it, the people all stood up. Ezra praised the Lord, the great God; and all the people lifted their hands and responded, Amen! Amen! Then they bowed and worshiped the Lord with their faces to the ground. They read from the Book of the Law, making it clear and giving the meaning so that the people could understand what was being read. Day after day, from the first day to the last, Ezra read from the Book of the Law of God."

2 Samuel 22:31: "As for God, his way is perfect: The Lord's word is flawless; he shields all who take refuge in him."

Deuteronomy 6:6-9: "These commandments that I give you today are to be upon your hearts. Impress them on your children. Talk about them when you sit at home and when you walk along the road, when you lie down and when you get up. Tie them as symbols on your hands and bind them on your foreheads. Write them on the door frames of your houses and on your gates."

Deuteronomy 8:3: "He humbled you, causing you to hunger and then feeding you with manna, which neither you nor your ancestors had known, to teach you that man does not live on bread alone but on every word that comes from the mouth of the Lord."

ADDITIONAL NOTES

Chapter 8
Jesus Is 100 Percent God

*W*hen Jesus spent time with his disciples in the region of Caesarea, he asked them, "Who do people say the Son of Man is?' They replied, 'Some say John the Baptist, others say Elijah, and still others, Jeremiah or one of the prophets'" (Matthew 16:13). We know from biblical history that these men were powerful preachers and prophets for God. They spoke the truth with conviction and many of them were subsequently put to death because of their unwillingness to soften God's message. These men were greatly esteemed by the Jews of Jesus's day. Yet Jesus was much greater than any of them.

He then turned the question to his best friends and asked them, "But what you about you? Who do you say I am?' Peter said, 'The Christ, the Son of the living God'" (v. 15). Jesus commended Peter for his response because he was correct. Every person must answer Jesus's question, "Who do you say I am?" Each disciple of Jesus would be wise to go on a personal quest to answer this question. If we want to be his followers, we must be willing to stake our lives on the belief that Jesus is God. Several first-century Christians who were unwilling to renounce Jesus as their God and Savior and hail Caesar as Lord, were tossed to the lions or burned with tar in Nero's garden.[1]

When you make Jesus your Lord, it requires a belief that he

is 100 percent God—no exceptions. If we expect to make it to heaven, this is an essential element of faith. In John 8:24, Jesus told the Jews, "If you do not believe that I am the one I claim to be, you will indeed die in your sins." Whom did Jesus claim to be? In the verses below, I make the case that he emphatically claimed to be deity—God in the flesh. The Jews wanted to kill Jesus throughout his earthly ministry because of his radical, but true, claims. He was not a god, as some religions claim, or an apparition. Jesus was not simply a good moral teacher or a philosophical guru. He was fully God, who lived fully as a human. If we do not believe this, according to Jesus himself, *we will die in our sins separated from God.*

He claims to be God:

John 10:30–35: "I and the Father are one.' Again the Jews picked up stones to stone him, but Jesus said to them, 'I have shown you many great miracles from the Father. For which of these do you stone me?' 'We are not stoning you for any of these, replied the Jews, but for blasphemy, **because you, a mere man claim to be God**'" (emphasis mine).

John 1:1;14: "In the beginning was the Word, and the Word was with God, **and the Word was God**. The Word became flesh and made his dwelling among us" (emphasis mine).

John 1:18 "No one has ever seen God, but God…"

John 5:16–18: "So, because Jesus was doing these on the Sabbath, the Jews persecuted him. Jesus said to them, 'My Father is always at his work to this very day, and I, too, am working.' For this reason the Jews tried all the harder to kill him; not only was breaking the Sabbath, but he was even calling God his own Father, **making himself equal with God**" (emphasis mine).

John 8:56–59: 'Your father Abraham rejoiced at the thought
of seeing my day; he saw it and was glad.' 'You are not yet
fifty years old, the Jews said to him, and you have seen
Abraham!' 'I tell you the truth,' Jesus answered, 'before
Abraham was born, **I am!'** At this the picked up stones
to stone him" (emphasis mine).

Exodus 3:13–14: "Moses said to God, 'Suppose I go the
Israelites and say to them, "The God of your fathers has
sent me to you," and they ask me, "What is his name?"
Then what shall I tell them?' **God said to Moses, 'I am
who I am**. This is what you are to say to the Israelites: **I
am has sent me to you**'" (emphasis mine).

John 5:46: "If you believed Moses, you would believe me, for
he wrote about me."

Note: Jesus is telling the Jews that he was the I am who spoke
with Moses at the bush! It was Jesus, who said to Moses,
'Do not come any closer. Take off your sandals, for the
place where you are standing is holy ground" (Exodus
3:5). The great I am the Jews esteemed in Moses' day
was standing before them, and they would not accept it!

Worshipped As God

The Jews were fanatical about how God should be worshiped.
The first three commandments center around the concept of one
God, and no one should come between the individual and him.
The devout Jews lived to worship the one true God of the Old
Testament. The fact that Jesus, a Jew, accepted worship from
his followers indicates that he claimed to be God. We don't see
Jesus pushing people away when they worshipped him. If he
were not God, he would not have embraced the worship that
was given him! Yet, whenever any of the apostles were given
reverential treatment, they adamantly refused to accept this form

of praise (Acts 10:24; 14:1–18), because they weren't God and never claimed to be.

> Luke 4:8: "Jesus answered, 'It is written: **'Worship the Lord your God ... only'**'" (emphasis mine).
>
> Luke 24:52 "When he had led them out to the vicinity of Bethany, he lifted up his hands and blessed them. While he was blessing them, he left them and was taken up into heaven. **Then they worshiped him** and returned to Jerusalem with great joy. And they stayed continually at the temple, praising God" (emphasis mine).
>
> John 9:35–38: "Jesus heard that they had thrown him out, and when he found him, he said, 'do you believe in the Son of Man?' 'Who is he, sir? The man asked. Tell me so that I may believe in him.' Jesus said, 'You have now seen him; in fact he is the one speaking with you.' Then the man said, 'Lord, I believe, **and he worshiped him**'" (emphasis mine).
>
> Matthew 28:9 "Suddenly Jesus met them. 'Greetings,' he said. They came to him, clasped his feet **and worshiped him**" (emphasis mine).
>
> Matthew 28:16–17 "Then the eleven disciples went to Galilee, to the mountain where Jesus had told them to go. When they saw him, **they worshiped him**..." (emphasis mine).
>
> John 20:28: "Thomas said to him, 'My Lord and my God.'"
>
> **Note:** What does Jesus say in his response to Thomas in verse 29? "Because you have seen me you have believed." What did Thomas believe? He believed that Jesus was his Lord and God!! Jesus goes on to say, "Blessed are those who have not seen and yet have believed." We too need to believe and worship Jesus the same way Thomas did: as our Lord and God.

Matthew 14:33 "'Those who were in the boat **worshiped him**, saying, 'Truly you are the Son of God'" (emphasis mine).

John 1:29; 35 "'The next day John saw Jesus coming toward him and said, 'Look, the **Lamb of God**...The next day John was there again with two of his disciples. When he saw Jesus passing by, he said, 'Look, the **Lamb of God'**" (emphasis mine)!

1Peter 1:19 "...but with the precious blood of *Christ, a lamb* without blemish or defect" (emphasis mine).

Note: Jesus is clearly portrayed as the Lamb of God, our perfect sin sacrifice. He deserves our worship because he is God. Notice the kind of worship that was given to the Lamb in heaven.

Revelation 5:6; 9; 11-14

> Then I **saw a Lamb**, looking as if it had been slain, standing in the center of the throne, encircled by the four living creatures and the elders. And they sang a new song: 'You are worthy to take the scroll and open its seals, because you were slain, and with your blood you purchased men for God from every tribe and language and people and nation.'
>
> Then I looked and heard the voice of many angels, numbering thousands upon thousands, and ten thousand times ten thousand. They encircled the throne and the living creatures and the elders. In a loud voice they sang:

Worthy is the Lamb, who was slain, to receive power and wealth and wisdom and strength and honor and glory and praise!

Then I heard every creature in heaven and on earth and under the earth and on the sea, and all that is in them, singing:

To **him who sits on the throne** *(God the Father)* and to **the Lamb** be praise and honor and glory and power, forever and ever!

The four living creatures said, 'Amen,' and the elders **fell down and worshiped** (emphasis mine).

Note: Jesus is God! Let us worship him with praise and adoration.

Equal with the Father

The terms *God* and *Father* are used interchangeably by Jesus throughout the gospel of John. They are one and the same. When you see Jesus, you see the Father, who he claimed was the God of the Jews.

John 8:54b: "**My Father, whom you claim as your God**, is the one who glorifies me" (emphasis mine). He was speaking with the Jews.

John 6:46 "No one has seen the Father except the one who is from God; only he has seen the Father."

John 16:27-28: "No, the Father himself loves you because you have loved me and have believed that **I came from God. I came from the Father** and entered the world;

now I'm leaving the world and going back to the Father"
(emphasis mine).

John 12:45: "The Jesus cried out, 'When a man believes in
me, he does not believe in me only but in the one who
sent me. When he looks at me, he sees the one who
sent me.'"

John 14:8–10: "Philip said, 'Lord, show us the Father and that
will be enough for us. Jesus answered: Don't you know
me, Phillip, even after I have been among you such a long
time? Anyone who seen me has seen the Father.'"

John 10:29: "My Father, who has given them to me, is greater
than all; no one can snatch them out of my Father's hand.
I and the Father are one."

God Forgives

Another piece of evidence proving that Jesus is God is his
power to forgive sins. As a Jew who attended synagogue on a
regular basis, Jesus was familiar with passages such as Isaiah 43:25:
"I, even I, am he who blots out your transgressions, for my own
sake, and remembers your sins no more." Over in Micah 7:18 it
says, "Who is a God like you, who pardons sins and forgives the
transgression of the remnant of his inheritance?" Jesus, as well as
the Jews, knew that only God had the power to forgive sins. On
one occasion at the house of Simon, a woman was anointing Jesus
with perfume. Jesus received this marvelous gesture that honored
him. At the end of this interaction between Jesus, the "sinful
woman," and Simon, Jesus turned to the woman and said, "Your
sins are forgiven." The other guests murmured among themselves,
"Who is this who even forgives sins?" (Luke 7:48–49). He is Jesus
of Nazareth, the Savior of the world, who came as the Lamb of
God to forgive the world of sin.

On another occasion, Jesus was moved to compassion when
a paralytic man was being lowered down from a hole in the roof

of a house, coming to rest at Jesus's feet. His friends had created a hole in the roof because there was no other way for them to get to Jesus because of the thick crowd. They were desperate to help their friend be healed. Jesus was amazed by their determination. "When Jesus saw their faith, he said to the paralytic, 'Son, your sins are forgiven.' Now some teachers of the law were sitting there, thinking to themselves, 'why does this fellow talk like that? He's blaspheming! Who can forgive sins but God alone?'" (Mark 2:5–7). Jesus went on to prove his claim to deity by healing the man of his paralysis. He not only forgave the man of his sins but also substantiated his claim to be God by healing the man! Jesus could forgive people of their sins because he was God in the flesh!

The thief on the cross is another beautiful picture of Jesus offering forgiveness of sins. Just before Jesus died, the repentant thief's heart was moved, and he said to Jesus, "'Remember me when you come into your kingdom.' Then Jesus answered him, 'I tell you the truth, today you will be with me in paradise'" (Luke 23:42–43). This is a magnificent portrait of our gracious God and Savior showing mercy and forgiveness. Only God can forgive sins! Jesus is God. While Jesus was alive he was able to *verbally* forgive sins. Since we don't hear the literal voice of Jesus any longer, he's given us a new way to find forgiveness of sins (see chapter twelve).

What others said about him.

Let's look at other passages found in the New Testament about Jesus being God. A person has to try really hard to ignore the testimony shared by the writers of scripture in the N.T.

> Romans 9:5: "'Theirs are the patriarchs, and from them is traced the human ancestry of Christ, **who is God** over all, forever praised!"
>
> Titus 2:13: "… while we wait for the blessed hope-the glorious appearing **of our great God and Savior, Jesus Christ**

who gave himself for us to redeem us from all wickedness and to purify for himself a people that are his very own, eager to do what is good" (emphasis mine).

Philippians 2:5–6: "Your attitude should be the same as that of Christ Jesus: **Who being in very nature God**" (emphasis mine).

Colossians 1:15: "He is the image of the invisible God."

Hebrews 1:8: "But about the Son he **(God)** says, 'Your throne O God, will last for ever and ever" (emphasis mine).

1 Peter 1:1: "Simon Peter, a servant and apostle of Jesus Christ, To those who through the righteousness **of our God and Savior Jesus Christ** have received a faith as precious as ours" (emphasis mine).

1 John 5:20: "We know also that the Son of God has come and has given us understanding, so that we may know him who is true. And we are in him who is true-even in his Son Jesus Christ. **He is the true God and eternal life**" (emphasis mine).

Acts 4:12 "Salvation is found in no one else, for there is no other name under heaven given to men by which we must be saved."

ADDITIONAL NOTES

Chapter 9
Jesus Was 100 Percent Human

*A*s shown in the prior chapter, Jesus is God. When he walked the earth, he was not only 100 percent God, he was also 100 percent human. His experience as a human was the same as yours and mine. God does not leave this up for debate. As his disciples, we must believe he was fully God and fully man. Otherwise, Jesus has some very strong words for us. "Every Spirit that acknowledges that Jesus Christ has come in the flesh is from God, but every spirit that does not acknowledge Jesus is not from God" (1 John 4:2–3). We must acknowledge his humanity or we will never connect with him on a personal level the way we should.

It gives me great comfort to know that Jesus can relate to the temptations I battle with daily. He overcame them. Many times I fail; however, knowing that he suffered when he was tempted yet was victorious motivates me to keep fighting the battle against sin. He wants us to know that he understands our struggle with fleshly temptations. However, he not only understands our struggle, but also he is able to help us overcome them too! "We have one who has been tempted in every way, just as we are—yet was without sin. For surely it is not angels he helps, but Abraham's descendants. For this reason he had to be made like his brothers in every way . . . because he himself suffered when he was tempted, he is able to help those who are being tempted" (Hebrews 4:15; 2:17–18). Jesus wants us to understand his humanity so that we will be comforted by his compassion regarding our temptations. He doesn't excuse our sin, but he understands we are in a constant battle to remain pure. We can overcome as he did, but we need his power in us (John 15:5).

He wasn't anesthetized from pain and suffering. He hurt just like you and me. When he heard that one of his best friends had died, he suffered emotionally, just as we do at the loss loved ones. He hungered for a good meal, thirsted for water, and became tired after exerting himself. He was sad on occasion. He cried. He experienced righteous anger. He suffered disappointment and celebrated at weddings. He sang. He took time to relax. He was one of us in every way! Doesn't it make you happy to know that Jesus calls us his brother and sister (Hebrews 2:11)?

What challenges do you struggle with? What temptations do you suffer to overcome? What hardship are you going through? Jesus can relate! The Bible says that he was tempted in every way, just as you are! His was not an easy life. In fact, his was the most difficult life ever lived! If he had failed even once, he would have failed all of humanity from the beginning of time. There would be no heaven for us. How's that for pressure? I'm thankful he can identify with us on a human level. This fact alone should bring us closer to him.

> John 1:14: "The Word became flesh." *Who was the Word?* John 1:1 says, "The Word was God."
> Note: God became a human, and embraced all the nuances of humanity, except he never sinned!
> 2 John 1:7: "Many deceivers, who do not acknowledge Jesus Christ as coming in the flesh, have gone out into the world. Any such person is the deceiver and the antichrist."
> John 11:35: "Jesus wept."

Matthew 4:2: "After fasting forty days and forty nights, he was hungry."

Matthew 26:38: "Then he said to them, 'My soul is overwhelmed with sorrow to the point of death.'"

Luke 22:44: "And being in anguish, he prayed more earnestly, and his sweat was like drops of blood falling to the ground."

John 4:6; 7: "Jacob's well was there, and Jesus, tired as he was from the journey, sat down by the well. When a Samaritan woman came to draw water, Jesus said to her, 'will you give me a drink?'"

John 19:28: "Later, knowing that all was now completed, and so that the scripture would be fulfilled, Jesus said, 'I am thirsty.'"

Galatians 4:4: "But when the time had fully come, God sent his son, born of a woman, born under law…"

I Timothy 1:2:5: "For there is one God, and one mediator also between God and men, *the man* Christ Jesus."

ADDITIONAL NOTES

Chapter 10
We Did What?

We missed the mark. That's what sin is—missing the mark of perfection.

Sometimes we aim for the bull's-eye (perfection), and we miss. The area between the arrow's mark and the bull's-eye is called sin. Perhaps we desire to do right, but then the desire to do wrong becomes more persuasive, and we act accordingly. This is sin. Other times, we don't even acknowledge the truth about a standard of perfection (God's Word) or the prick of conscience (guilt), and we dive headlong into what we know is wrong. This, too, is sin.

The scary thing about sin is that there comes a time when a conscience becomes seared to the point of not feeling the prick of guilt when doing wrong (1 Timothy 4:2). For example, let's say one year you cheated on your taxes and you felt terribly guilty. No threat of an audit came from the IRS, so the next year you cheated again. You sensed a bit of guilt, but it was easier to push aside, reasoning that the IRS is certainly no bastion of honesty. And so it goes every year around tax time. Cheating on your taxes then becomes a way of life, and now you have no guilt. In fact, you easily justify it as something that is actually good. Your conscience has become seared. It doesn't recognize wrongdoing, much less admit to it. If you have gone from feeling guilty to good about something, I hope the alarm bells go off.

Sin is scary for a lot of reasons. It is deceptive. It is cunning. It is insidious. Many times it feels so good, even right . . . for the moment. We can lose touch with just how destructive sin is. If we do not feel the sting of guilt when we sin, our hearts are becoming, or have become, hard. After all, Jesus sent the Spirit "to *convict the world of guilt* in regard to sin and righteousness and judgment" (John 16:8). It is good for us to feel guilty when we sin! It's an internal, spiritual alarm system. It should drive us to our knees in reliance on God. The apostles did not hold back in making others feel guilty! "We gave you strict orders not to teach in this name, the high priest said. Yet you have filled Jerusalem with your teaching and are determined to make us guilty of this man's blood" (Acts 5:28).

As we will see in the next study, sin nailed Jesus on the cross. Missing the mark, whether intentionally or unintentionally, caused Jesus to be sacrificed. Until you and I see the gruesomeness of our sin, we will never fully appreciate the greatness of Jesus's love (Luke 7:47).

The word *sin* isn't some religious word to yawn at. Rather, it is a very serious condition that plagues all of humanity. The Bible says the wage of sin is death. When you work, you expect a wage, right? You work an hour, you expect whatever that wage is for the hour. Guess what wage you earn when you sin? Death: eternal separation from God (Romans 6:23). All of us fall short of God's glory (3:23). No matter how saintly one may appear, they, too, fall short of perfection. Aside from Jesus, *not a single person* who has ever lived has not sinned.

We not only dabble in sin, we swim in it. We bask in it. We get lots of pleasure from it. How sad it is when we choose death over life. God desires for us to be with him for eternity. Instead, too often we love our sin more than God. *All of us* need help with our sin problem. Finding the antidote is critical. It is the difference between life and death! Sin separates. Sin hurts—it hurt us, it hurts others, and it hurts God. He weeps when we choose sin over him. As a matter fact, sin is such a deadly disease that Jesus left the comfort of heaven to become a human so that we could be cured. We need to be forgiven. I encourage you to read Psalm 51. In fact, this is a good psalm to memorize.

We need to understand that unless we change, reverse course, and find forgiveness from God, there is no hope of eternal life (2 Corinthians 7:8-11 and Romans 2:4-5). Even after 30 years, when I read the passages below, I realize how desperately I need God and his forgiveness.

Galatians 5:19: "The acts of the sinful nature are obvious: sexual immorality, impurity and debauchery; idolatry and witchcraft; hatred, discord, jealousy, fits of rage, selfish ambition, dissensions, factions and envy; drunkenness, orgies, and the like. I warn you, as I did before, that those who live like this will not inherit the kingdom of God."

Ephesians 5:3-7: "But among you there must not be even a hint of sexual immorality, or of any kind of impurity, or of greed, because these are improper for God's holy people. Nor should there be obscenity, foolish talk or coarse joking, which are out of place, but rather thanksgiving. For of this you can be sure: No immoral, impure or greedy person-such a man is an idolater-has any inheritance in the in the kingdom of Christ and of God. Let no one deceive you with empty words, for because of such things God's wrath comes on those who are disobedient. Therefore do not be partners with them."

1 Corinthians 6:9-11: "Do you not know that the wicked will not inherit the kingdom of God? Do not be deceived: Neither the sexually immoral nor idolaters nor adulterers nor male prostitutes nor homosexual offenders nor thieves nor the greedy nor drunkards nor slanderers nor swindlers will inherit the kingdom of God. *And that is what some of you were.* But you

were washed, you were sanctified, you were justified in the name of the Lord Jesus Christ and by the Spirit of our God" (emphasis mine).

Romans 1:24-31: "Therefore God gave them over in the sinful desires of their hearts to sexual impurity for the degrading of their bodies with one another. They exchanged the truth of God for a lie, and worshiped and served created things rather than the Creator-who is forever praised. Amen.

Because of this, God gave them over to shameful lusts. Even their women exchanged natural relations for unnatural ones. In the same way the men also abandoned natural relations with women and were inflamed with lust for one another. Men committed indecent acts with other men, and received in themselves the due penalty for their perversion.

Furthermore, since they did not think it worthwhile to retain the knowledge of God, he gave them over to a depraved mind, to do what ought not to be done. They have become filled with every kind of wickedness, evil, greed and depravity. They are full of envy, murder, strife, deceit and malice. They are gossips, slanderers, God-haters, insolent, arrogant and boastful; they invent ways of doing evil; they disobey their parents; they are senseless, faithless, heartless, ruthless. Although they know God's righteous decree that those who do such things deserve death, they not only continue to these very things but also approve of those who practices them."

James 4:17 "Anyone, then, who knows the good he ought to do and doesn't do it, sins."

Romans 14:23 "But the man who has doubts is condemned if he eats, because his eating is not from faith; *and everything that does not come from faith is sin*" (emphasis mine).

Where do we fall short? What sins are we guilty of? There is a remedy for our sin problem. The good news is found in chapters 11 and 12.

ADDITIONAL NOTES

Chapter 11
Jesus Did What?

*J*esus allowed himself to be killed, and we were the ones who murdered him. As shocking as this sounds, it's true! Many people have a hard time believing that they nailed Jesus to the cross. Some folks blame the Jews for the death of Jesus, and others blame the Romans; but the fact is, all mankind is responsible for his death. Each of us drove the nails through his hands and feet. You and I punched him in the face. Together we spit on him, drove the crown of thorns deep into his scalp, and beat him with rods. How do I know? Because each of us sinned (see chapter 10). Jesus had to die for our sins or else we would have no hope to be with him and his Father for eternity. Jesus came to save you from your sin. He came for me. He came for the world. Every human who has lived or will live is responsible for his death. He was the Father's perfect sin sacrifice for us! "God made him who had no sin to be sin for us, so that in him we might become the righteousness of God" (2 Corinthians 5:21).

Only a perfect human sacrifice was good enough to appease the Father, turn away his wrath against us, and have him smile down upon us. Peter wrote, "He himself bore our sins in his body on the tree, so that we might die to sins and live for righteousness, by his wounds you have been healed" (1 Peter 2:24).). John also says, "But you know that he appeared so that he might take away our sins. And in him is no sin" (1 John 3:5). If Jesus never left heaven to willingly lay down his perfect life for you and me, we would have no hope. "But God demonstrates his own love for us in this: While we were still sinners, Christ died for us" (Romans 5:8). Jesus never committed a single sin. He never lied. He never cheated on a test, his taxes, or in any other way. He never disobeyed his parents. He never used foul language. He never had a bad thought about anyone. He never lusted after a woman. He was never impure in his thoughts, actions, or motives. He never complained. He never sinned! Scripture is clear on this point. "He committed no sin, and no deceit was found in his mouth" (1 Peter 2:22). If anyone could point out sin in Jesus's life, it would've been Peter. Yet he, too, died on a cross because he would not deny the truth that Jesus committed no sin!

Jesus was the perfect sacrifice for you and me. He was tempted as we are. He struggled intensely not to sin *even once throughout his life, and he was victorious*! "We have one has been tempted in every way, just as we are—yet was without sin" (Hebrews 4:15).

Isn't this the greatest news? He is our antidote to be forgiven of all our sin! Every Christian should know when he or she received forgiveness of past, present and future sin (more on this in chapter twelve). If you are a believer in Christ, no doubt you know the day, maybe even the hour, when his blood washed away your sin and you received forgiveness as well as the Holy Spirit.

I have to often remind myself of a couple of scriptures about embracing God's forgiveness. I recently turned the ripe old age of fifty, and the older I get, the more I see the magnitude of my sin. At times it is hard for me to embrace God's grace. I feel like I'm too big of a sinner for God to love me. I've been a disciple since 1987, and I still wrestle with the same sin I struggled with back then. I sometimes wonder, does God still forgive me?

But then the apostle Peter comes to mind when he asked Jesus what I'm sure all of us would probably ask if we were in the company of Jesus—especially if our siblings were with us:

"Lord, how many times should I forgive my brother? Maybe no more than seven times?" And Jesus said, "Peter you have it all wrong. Not seven times, but seventy times seven" (Matthew 18:21, author's paraphrase). Jesus doesn't mean a literal 490 times. That would be hard enough. Actually, Jesus turns up the dial a few notches and means, *"There is no limit to the amount of times you forgive your brother (sister) who asks you to forgive him."*[1] Whoa. I can envision Peter falling off his chair. However, I take great comfort in those words from Jesus. If he holds us to this standard, isn't his love, grace, mercy, and forgiveness so much greater than ours? Of course it is! Another scripture I often recite in prayer is "If we confess our sins, he is faithful and just and will forgive us of our sins and purify from us from all unrighteousness" (1 John 1:9). What an amazing promise!

Yes, you and I nailed Jesus to the cross. Yes, he is our only hope to make it to heaven. Yes, without him we would never be forgiven of the gross sin we often commit. Let's be compelled to be our best by embracing the love of Jesus displayed on the cross. Let's make him our best friend.

1 John 2:1: "My dear children, I write this to you so that you will not sin. But if anybody does sin, we have one who speaks to the Father in our defense-Jesus Christ, the Righteous One."

1 John 2:2: "He is the atoning sacrifice for our sins, and not only for ours but also for the sins of the whole world.

Isaiah 43:25: "I, even I am he who blots out your transgressions, for my own sake, and remembers your sins no more."

Psalm 32:1: "Blessed is he whose transgressions are forgiven, who sins are covered."

Psalm 103:3: "Praise the Lord, O my soul; all my inmost being, praise his holy name. Praise the Lord, O my soul, and forget not all his benefits-who forgives all your sins..."

Psalm 103:10: "He does not treat us as our sins deserve or repay us according to our iniquities."

Psalm 103:12: "As far as the east from the west, so far has he removed our transgressions from us."

Note: When we travel east and do not turn around, we will continue east forever. The east and west will never meet. That's how God treats our sins once we come into contact with Jesus's blood (See chapter 12).

Isaiah 1:18: "Come now, let us reason together, says the Lord. Though your sins are like scarlet, they shall be white as snow; though they are red as crimson, they shall be like wool."

Daniel 9:9: "The Lord our God is merciful and forgiving, even though we have rebelled against him."

ADDITIONAL NOTES

Chapter 12
New Creation

I thought I'd share a few scriptures about the blessings we receive when we get into Christ Jesus. Once we understand what we did to Jesus, and what he did for us, prayerfully we are motivate to find out *how we get into Christ,* and how we become a new creation. One of the most important questions we need to ask in our quest to know God is, "How do we get into Christ?" As you'll see from scripture, how we answer this question determines our spiritual destiny, and gaining access to many spiritual blessings!

> Galatians 6:15: "Neither circumcision nor uncircumcision means anything; **what counts is a new creation**" (emphasis mine).
> 2 Corinthians 5:17: "Therefore, if anyone is **in Christ he is a new creation**; the old has gone, the new has come" (emphasis mine).

According to Paul, what counts in life is becoming a new creation...experiencing a new birth. Jesus spoke about a new birth in John 3:1–3. He says we must be born again - of water and the spirit - to see and enter the kingdom of heaven. Those who are born again become a new creation, the old person is gone. Paul gives additional insight into Jesus's words by letting us know we become a new creation by getting into Christ. There is no other way.

If we want to be a new creation, *we must figure out how to get into Christ.* Thankfully, the scriptures are very clear about how to do this. Let's see what Paul said about how we get into Christ, how we become a new creation, and how we are born again.

> Galatians 3:27: "For all of you who were **_baptized into_ Christ** have clothed yourselves with Christ" (emphasis mine).
> Romans 6:3-4: "Or don't you know that all of us who were **_baptized into_ Christ Jesus** were baptized into his death? We were therefore buried with him through baptism into death in order that, just as Christ was raised from the dead through the glory of the Father, we too may live a new life" (emphasis mine).

Presto! There's the answer to how we get into Christ. According to scripture, *the only way we get into Christ* is through baptism (fully immersed in water). We don't pray ourselves into Christ. We don't will ourselves into Christ. We don't believe ourselves into Christ. Baptism isn't merely an act to pledge our conscience to God (1 Peter 3:21). It is *essential* for salvation. The point in time we become a new creation (born again), receive forgiveness of sins, and gain entrance into the kingdom of God *is when we get baptized into Christ.*

Below are some additional passages about the blessings we receive when we get into Christ.

Note: The words "in Christ Jesus" in the passages below are in bold letters and my emphasis.

1 John 3:5: "And **in him** is no sin."

Note: A simple phrase rich in meaning! There is no sin in Jesus. When we get baptized into Jesus, we have no sin. It doesn't mean we will never sin again. It just means that we've been washed, we've be cleansed from all our sin. When God looks at us, he sees us without blemish and free from accusation (Colossians 1:22)!!

> Colossians 1:13: "For he has rescued us from the dominion of darkness and brought us into the kingdom of the Son he loves, **in whom** we have redemption, the forgiveness of sins"
>
> Ephesians 1:7: "**In him** we have redemption through his blood, the forgiveness of sins."
>
> Ephesians 4:32: "Be kind and compassionate to one another, forgiving each other, just as **in Christ Jesus** God forgave you."
>
> Romans 8:1: "Therefore, there is now no condemnation for those who are **in Christ Jesus**."
>
> Romans 6:23: "For the wages of sin is death, but the gift of God is eternal life **in Christ Jesus** our Lord."
>
> Romans 8:38-39: "For I am convinced that neither death nor life, neither angels nor demons, neither the present nor the future, nor any powers, neither height nor depth, nor anything else in all creation, will be able to separate us from the love of God that is **in Christ** Jesus our Lord."
>
> Romans 14:14: "As one who is **in the Lord Jesus**, I am fully convinced that no food is unclean in itself."
>
> Romans 15:7: "Greet Adronicus and Junias, my relatives who have been in prison with me. They are outstanding among the apostles, and they were **in Christ** before I was."
>
> 1 Corinthians 1:4: "I always thank God for you because of his grace given you **in Christ** Jesus.'
>
> 1 Corinthians 15:22: "For as in Adam all die, so **in Christ** all will be made alive."

2 Corinthians 1:20: "For no matter how many promises God has made, they are 'Yes' **in Christ**."

2 Corinthians 1:21: "Now it is God who makes both us and you stand firm **in Christ**."

2 Corinthians 3:13-14: "We are not like Moses, who would put a veil over his face to keep the Israelites from gazing at it while the radiance was fading away. But their minds were made dull, for to this day the same veil remains when the old covenant is read. It has not been removed, because only **in Christ** is it taken away."

2 Corinthians 5:21: "God made him who had no sin to be sin for us, so that **in him** we might become the righteousness of God."

Galatians 3:28: "There is neither Jew nor Greek, slave nor free, male nor female, for you are all one **in Christ Jesus**."

Galatians 5:6 "For **in Christ Jesus** neither circumcision nor uncircumcision has any value."

Ephesians 1:3-4: "Praise be to the God and Father of our Lord Jesus Christ, who has blessed us in the heavenly realms with every spiritual blessing **in Christ**. For he chose us **in him** before the creation of the world to be holy and blameless in his sight."

Ephesians 1:11: "**In him** we were also chosen..."

Ephesians 1:13: "And you also were included **in Christ** when you heard the word of truth, the gospel of your salvation."

Ephesians 2:6: "And God raised us up with Christ and seated us with him in the heavenly realms **in Christ Jesus**."

Ephesians 2:10: "For we are God's workmanship, created **in Christ Jesus** to do good works, which God prepared in advance for us to do."

Ephesians 2:13: "But now **in Christ Jesus** you who once were far away have been brought near through the blood of Christ."

Ephesians 2:22: "And **in him** you too are being built together to become a dwelling in which God lives by his Spirit."

Ephesians 3:6: "This mystery is that through the gospel the Gentiles are heirs together with Israel, members together of one body, and sharers together in the promise **in Christ Jesus**."

Ephesians 3:12: "**In him** and through faith in him we may approach God with freedom and confidence."

Ephesians 4:21: "Surely you heard of him and were taught **in him** accordance with the truth that is **in Jesus**."

Ephesians 5:8: "For you were once darkness, but now you are light **in the Lord**."

Philippians 1:26: "So that through my being with you again your joy **in Christ Jesus** will overflow on account of me."

Philippians 3:3: "...who glory **in Christ Jesus**..."

Philippians 3:14: "I press on toward the goal to win the prize for which God has called me heavenward **in Christ Jesus**."

Philippians 4:6-7: "Do not be anxious about anything, but in everything, by prayer and petition, with thanksgiving, present your requests to God. And the peace of God, which transcends all understanding, will guide your hearts and minds **in Christ Jesus**."

Philippians 4:19: "And my God will meet all your needs according to his glorious riches **in Christ Jesus.**"

Philippians 4:21: "Greet all the saints **in Christ Jesus**."

Colossians 1:2: "To the holy and faithful brothers **in Christ** at Colosse."

Colossians 1:28: "We proclaim him, admonishing and teaching everyone with all wisdom, so that we may present everyone perfect **in Christ**."

Colossians 2:11: "**In him** you were also circumcised, in the putting off of the sinful nature, not with a circumcision done by the hands of men but with a circumcision by

Christ, having been buried with him in baptism and raised with him through your faith in the power of God, who raised him from the dead."

Colossians 2:16: 'Therefore do not let anyone judge you by what you eat or drink, or with regard to a religious festival, a New Moon celebration or a Sabbath day. These are a shadow of the things that were to come; **the reality, however, is found in Christ.**'

1 Thessalonians 5:16: "Be joyful always; pray continually; give thanks in all circumstances, for this is God's will for you **in Christ Jesus.**"

1 Timothy 1:14: "The grace of our Lord was poured out on me abundantly, along with the faith, and love that are **in Christ Jesus.**"

2 Timothy 1:1: "...according to the promise of life that is **in Christ Jesus.**"

2 Timothy 1:9 "This grace was given us **in Christ Jesus...**"

2 Timothy 2:1: "You then, my son, be strong in the grace that is **in Christ Jesus.**"

2 Timothy 2:10: "Therefore I endure everything for the sake of the elect, that they too may obtain the salvation that is **in Christ Jesus.**"

2 Timothy 3:12: "In fact, anyone who wants to live a godly life **in Christ Jesus** will be persecuted."

Philemon 1:6: "I pray that you may be active in sharing your faith, so that you will have a full understanding of every good thing we have **in Christ.**"

1 John 5:11: "And this is the testimony: God has given us eternal life, and this life is **in his Son.**"

Revelation 1:9: "I, John, your brother and companion in the sufferings and kingdom and patient endurance that are ours **in Jesus**, was on the island of Patmos because of the word of God and the testimony of Jesus."

Note: I have often wondered about Paul's words found in Romans 13:14, where he mentions being clothed with Christ: "Rather, clothe yourselves with the Lord Jesus Christ, and do not think about how to gratify the desires of the sinful nature." How do we clothe ourselves with Christ? At what point do we 'wear' Jesus? The scriptures once again give us the answer.

> Galatians 3:27: "For all of you who baptized into Christ have clothed yourselves with Christ."

When we get baptized into Christ, we are clothed with Christ. There is only one way we can be unclothed from Jesus: *if* we choose to renounce him and go back to the world (James 4:4). May it not be so!

In 2 Timothy 2:13, Paul also mentions a "trustworthy saying" that deserves full acceptance: "If we died with him, we will also live with him." Question, how do we die with him? *Answer:* Romans 6:4 "We were therefore buried with him through baptism into death in order that, just as Christ was raised from the dead through the glory of the Father, we too may live a new life." Another scripture confirming how we die with him is found in Colossians 2:12 "…having been buried with him in baptism and raised with him through your faith in the power of God, who raised him from the dead." Not only do we **die with him** in baptism, but we are also given **a new life** with him through baptism. Remember, the 'key' isn't baptism per se, but *in our faith in the power of God working through the waters of baptism*–which represents Jesus's blood–that allows us to be buried with Jesus, and come up a new creation.

Baptism is essential for salvation! It is the only way we are given a new life and become a new creation.

ADDITIONAL NOTES

Chapter 13
Follow Jesus

Before we become a new creation, we should know what it means to be a disciple of Jesus. What is the definition of *disciple?* It means to be a student or learner of the one you are following. Christians are Jesus's students. Jesus gave specific instructions of what it takes to be his follower.

Bible.org offers a good description:

> A disciple of Rabbi Jesus is one who totally surrenders to Him and His way of seeing and doing things. As such, a disciple comes with a willing desire to conform all aspects of his or her life to the authoritative Lordship of Jesus Christ. To Jesus, righteousness was a matter of the heart, not a codification of behavior. Furthermore, Jesus came to reveal further 'who God is and how God does things,' a favorite phrase of Dr. James C. Martin, co-Founder of Preserving Bible Times. Thus, a disciple of Jesus is one who is always asking Jesus, as revealed in Scripture, more about who God is as well as God's will and ways.[1]

Jesus's call to be his disciple is challenging. It is not easy to deny oneself. However, he is our Good Shepherd so he will guide us and take care of us. He will give each of us strength through his Spirit to live as he commands. When you make the decision to be his disciple, you are committing to thinking, living, and acting the way Jesus did (1 John 2:6). In return, Jesus will be by your side to comfort and lead you. He will be in you as the storms of life come. He said, "Come to me all you who are weary and burdened, and I will give you rest. Take my yoke upon you and learn from me, for I am gentle and humble in heart, and you will find rest for your souls. For my yoke is easy and burden is light" (Matthew 11:28–20). He is not a harsh taskmaster. He is always with us with arms wide open.

We should have a basic understanding of what it means to be a disciple of Jesus *before we get baptized*. "Therefore go and make disciples of all nations, baptizing them" (Matthew 28:19). This verse states that only Jesus's disciples should enter the waters of baptism. God warns of severe consequences for those who come to faith in Jesus, are baptized, begin the Christian journey, but then give up. He would rather us not start the race than to start and eventually quit. "If they have escaped the corruption of the world by knowing our Lord and Savior Jesus Christ and are again entangled in it and overcome, they are worse off at the end than they were at the beginning. It would have been better for them not to have known the way of righteousness, than to have known it and then turn their backs on the scared command that was passed on to them" (2 Peter 2:20–22). To follow Jesus is a life-long commitment. Know what this commitment entails before you wear the clothes of Jesus at baptism.

Let's figure out what it takes to be a life-long student of Jesus so we're not tempted to walk away when the road gets bumpy. We need to follow him no matter what difficult or overwhelming circumstances comes knocking. This is why Jesus prompts us to count the cost before we begin the race marked out for us (Luke 14:28). It's a long, arduous, and bumpy race. However, the blessings we receive during this journey far outweighs any obstacles we encounter. And what's more amazing is that when we cross the finish line, heaven awaits us!

Keep in mind, when you read the word *disciple* (as it relates to Jesus) in the New Testament, you're essentially reading the word *Christian* in today's vernacular (Acts 11:26). The disciples of Jesus were not called Christians until approximately AD 40. The term Christian was used in a derogatory sense when speaking about disciples of Jesus. However, over the course of time, Jesus followers came to be known as Christians. In modern times the term Christian has become watered down. In our world today, there are many different definitions of what it means to be a Christian. However, Jesus was very clear and specific about what it took to be one of his disciples! Below are a several verses (of many) that describes what it means to be his disciples

> Luke 14:25: "'Large crowds were traveling with Jesus, and turning to them he said: 'If anyone comes to me and does not hate his father and mother, his wife and children, his brothers and sisters – yes even his own life – **he cannot be my disciple**'" (emphasis mine). A parallel passage is found in Matthew 10:37 where Jesus says you must love him more than your father, mother, brother, etc...
>
> Luke 14:27: "And anyone who does not carry his cross and follow me **cannot be my disciple**" (emphasis mine).
>
> John 8:31: "'To the Jews who had believed him, Jesus said, 'If you hold to my teaching, you really are my disciples. Then you will know the truth, and the truth will set you free.'"
>
> John 14:15: "If you love me, you will obey what I command."
>
> John 15:10: "If you obey my commands you will remain in my love, just as I have obeyed my Father's commands and remain in his love."

Luke 11:1 "'One day Jesus was praying in a certain place. When he finished, one of his disciples said to him, 'Lord, teach us to pray, just as John taught his disciples.'"

Luke 9:57-62 "'As they were walking along the road, a man said to him, 'I will follow you wherever you go.' Jesus replied, 'Foxes have holes and the birds of the air have nests, but the Son of Man has no place to lay his head.' He said to another man, 'Follow me.' But the man replied, 'Lord, first let me go and bury my father.' Jesus said to him, 'Let the dead bury their own dead, but you go and proclaim the kingdom of God.' Still another said, 'I will follow you Lord; but first let me go back and say good-by to my family.' Jesus replied, 'No one who puts his hand to the plow and looks back is fit for service in the kingdom of God.'"

Luke 14:28-33: "Suppose one of you wants to build a tower. **Will he not first sit down and estimate the cost to see if he has enough money to complete it?** For if he lays the foundation and is not able to finish it, everyone who sees it will ridicule him, saying, 'this fellow began to build and was not able to finish.' Or suppose a king is about to go to war against another king. Will he not first sit down and consider whether he is able with ten thousand men to oppose the one coming against him with twenty thousand? If he is not able, he will send a delegation while the other is still a long way off and will ask for terms of peace. In the same way, any of you who does not give up everything he has **cannot be my disciple**'" (emphasis mine).

John 13:35: "By this all men will know that **you are my disciples**, if you love one another" (emphasis mine).

Luke 9:24: "For whoever wants to save his life will lose it, but whoever loses his life for me will save it. What good is it for a man to gain the whole world, and yet lose or forfeit his very self?"

Acts 9:36: "In Joppa there was a disciple named Tabitha (which, when translated, is Dorcas), who was always doing good and helping the poor."

Matthew 4:18: "'As Jesus was walking beside the Sea of Galilee, he saw two brothers, Simon called Peter and his brother Andrew. They were casting a net into the lake, for they were fishermen. 'Come, follow me,' Jesus said, 'and I will make you fishers of men.' At once they left their nets and followed him.'"

Matthew 28:19; 20: "Therefore go and make disciples of all nations baptizing them...teaching them to obey everything I have commanded you."

Note: The word 'go' is not a suggestion, but a command given by Jesus. As disciples, we must put into practice the command of introducing others to Jesus, so that they have an opportunity to become one of his disciples. Once a person makes the decision to be a baptized disciple, they are then commanded to *go* and make disciples. As we *go* and make disciples, the world will be won for Jesus. Amen!

Another instance where Jesus tells his disciples to 'go' is found in John 15:16. This chapter focuses on remaining in the vine and bearing fruit. Jesus calls us to have a life of impact (bearing fruit), while exhibiting the fruits of the Spirit such as love, joy, peace, patience, kindness, etc... He tell his apostles, "you did not choose me, but I chose you and *appointed you to go* and bear fruit-fruit that will last." (Emphasis mine). If Jesus is speaking merely of the fruits of the Spirit there is no need to 'go.' Instead, he is telling them to go impact the world for God's glory. There is no greater mission in life than to help people understand who Jesus is, and teach them how to get to heaven.

ADDITIONAL NOTES

Chapter 14
We Need Friends

*W*hen you begin your journey as a disciple of Jesus (a new creation), it is imperative to surround yourself with like-minded men and women. The Enemy wants to distract and destroy you. You can't see him. He's fierce. You can see the results of his carnage everywhere. His sole focus is to kill, maim, and destroy. He wants as many people as possible to die separated from God for all eternity. He knows his time is short, and he is angry (Revelation 12:2). We witness his destruction and fury every day as we read and listen to the news about the senseless murders and crimes. The apostle Peter said the devil is like a roaring lion looking for someone to devour (2 Peter 5:8). His hunger is never satisfied. He wants to take you down with him. According to www.dictionary.com, the definition of devour is, "To swallow or eat up hungrily, voraciously, or ravenously." He wants nothing more than for us to be isolated and alone. He wants us to think we can live the Christian life as a Lone Ranger, or being with people who have no desire to know God.

Can you imagine wanting to be a great athlete without spending lots of time with like-minded athletes and coaches? It would be challenging, if not impossible. However, if an athlete surrounds herself with friends who have the same athletic goals and encourage her to be her best, it provides motivation to remain focused on greatness.

The writer of Proverbs teaches, "As iron sharpens iron, so one man sharpens another" (Proverbs 27:17). This principal applies to all people. You need spiritual friends who will "sharpen" you to be your best at school or at work, to be your best for your family, friends, and, most importantly, for God. Paul wrote, "Bad company corrupts good character" (1 Corinthians 15:33). No matter how strong your character is, no matter how much you desire to be like Jesus, if you are not building best friendships with other disciples, you will have a tough time weathering the storms of life that are sure to strike (John 16:33). You need the encouragement of other disciples. They help you stay focused on the goal of becoming like Jesus.

Many people, Christians included, have a misconception of what church is. It's not some ornate building. It's not a conference center or cathedral with a sign out front that says CHURCH. Church is a group of disciples who help one another grow in our love for God and others. Church is getting (and giving) encouragement from brothers and sisters in Christ who call us to fix our eyes on the Author and Perfecter of our faith (Jesus). It is about building best friendships with followers of Jesus that lasts for eternity. The church is not a building; rather, the church is you, it is me, it is Jesus's disciples coming together to build one another up.

Do you ever feel like you attend church services just to say you went, to fulfill some kind of felt obligation? You arrive, you leave, and no one notices. You don't connect with anyone. You're not actively pursuing friendships with other followers, and no one is pursuing you, either. You listen to the sermons but then go back to living the way you want the other six days of the week. I've been there—even as a disciple of Jesus. It is not a good place to be. My walk with God suffered greatly. This isn't the way God intended for church to be lived. We should look forward to seeing our friends on Sundays, or any day disciples come together.

The church is called the body of Christ. As his followers, we constitute Jesus's body, of which he is the head (Ephesians 5:23). When believers gather as friends, or as the body of Christ, we should be thinking about how to put into practice the many "one another passages" found in Scripture. Let us continuously examine, reflect on, meditate, memorize, and put into practice the one another passages. It is a fun study. You can find one hundred one another verses in the New Testament: **http:// overviewbible.com/one-another-infographic/**

When we come together as the body of Jesus, we should be excited. We should look forward to seeing our friends as we love God together. Contrary to what many believe, being a member of the body of Jesus isn't optional. It's not an optional commitment. It's not something you do when you feel like it. If we do not belong to a body of believers, we lose connection with the head, who is Jesus (Colossian 2:18-19). If we don't have Jesus, we have nothing. We need the body and the body needs us!

1 Corinthians 12:27: "**Now you are the body of Christ**, and each of you is a part of it." (Emphasis mine).

Ephesians 5:29-30: "After all, no one ever hated his own body, but he feeds and cares for it, just as Christ does the church- **for we are members of his body**" (Emphasis mine).

Colossians 1:18: "And he is the head of the body, the church."

Ephesians 4:15-16: "Instead, speaking the truth in love, we will in all things grow up into him who is the Head, that is, Christ. From him the whole body, joined and held together by every supporting ligament, grows and builds itself up in love, as each part does its work.'

Ephesians 1:22: "And God placed all things under his feet and appointed him to be head over everything for the church, which is his body, the fullness of him who fills everything in every way."

1 Corinthians 12:13: "For we were all baptized by one Spirit **into one body...**"

Note: When we are totally immersed in water (baptism), not only do we get into Christ (the head), but we also get into his body (the church). According to scripture, without baptism, these two realities are not possible.

A couple of examples of one another passages:

John 13: "A new command I give you: love one another. As I have loved you, so you must love one another. By this, all men will know that you are my disciples if you love one another."

Hebrews 4:10: "Encourage one another daily..."

Here is the link with an infographic on the one another passages found in the scriptures.

http://overviewbible.com/one-another-infographic/

ADDITIONAL NOTES

Chapter 15
It Is True!

*Y*es, it is true! God loves you! He loves me. An amazing concept. The Creator of the universe has an undying love for us. He demonstrated the magnitude of his love by sending Jesus to free us from the destruction of sin and the fear of death. He made a way for us to live a joyful, confident, and full life. We are protected by the hands of Jesus and the Father (John 10:28-29). He gave us his Word to specify his love for us. Below I highlight ten verses that comfort my heart when I think about how much God loves me. I'm sure you have others that you can add. It is easy to generalize God's love but not fully grasp how deep and wide and high and personal his love is for you and me! He loves us individually, not *just* collectively, as a world. Yes, it is true!

> Psalm 17:8: "Keep me as the apple of your eye; hide me in the shadow of your wings…"
> **Note**: Wikipedia says that the phrase apple of my eye refers to something or someone that one cherishes above all others. https://en.m.wikipedia.org/wiki/Apple_of_my_eye
> Isaiah 49:15: "Can a mother forget the baby at her breast and have no compassion on the child she has borne? Though she may forget, I will not forget you."

Psalm 139:13-14: "For you created my inmost being; you knit me together in my mother's womb. I praise you because I am fearfully and wonderfully made; your works are wonderful, I know that full well."

Isaiah 49:16: "See, I have engraved you on the palms of my hands."

Zephaniah 3:17: "The Lord your God is with you, he is mighty save. He will take great delight in you, he will quiet you with his love, he will rejoice over you with singing."

1 Peter 5:7: "Cast your anxiety on him because he cares for you."

Isaiah 43:1-3: "Fear not, for I have redeemed you; I have summoned you by name; you are mine. When you pass through the rivers, they will not sweep over you. When you walk through the fire, you will not be burned; the flames will not set you ablaze. For I am the Lord, your God, the Holy One of Israel, your Savior."

Isaiah 41:10: "So do not fear, for I am with you; do not be dismayed, for I am your God. I will strengthen you and help you; I will uphold you with my righteous hand."

Deuteronomy 7:6: "For you are a holy people to the Lord your God. The Lord your God has chosen you out of all the peoples on the face of the earth to be his treasured possession."

Jeremiah 29:11: "For I know the plans I have for you, declares the Lord, plans to prosper you and not to harm you, plans to give you a hope and a future."

ADDITIONAL NOTES

Chapter 16
His Amazing Prayer Life

The fact that Jesus prayed, convinces me that I need to pray even more. Jesus was God, and if there was someone who didn't need to pray during his time on earth, it was Jesus. He resurrected people from the dead, he multiplied bread and fish, silenced demons, and was always doing kind acts for people. Why did Jesus need to pray? After all, he was God. If Jesus didn't believe in the power prayer, he wouldn't have done it! If the disciples didn't see a marked changed as a result of Jesus prayer life, they wouldn't have asked him, "Lord, teach us how to pray..." (Luke 11:1). Can you imagine listening to Jesus pray? I'm sure it would move us to pray more than we do. The great news is, he left us a glimpse into his prayer life to imitate and learn from.

As we will see from scripture, it was because of his prayer life that he was able to accomplish amazing miracles, overcome the onslaught of temptation, and not get pulled into ways of this world. If Jesus often desired to be with the Father, we should have this same goal. The ruler of this world does everything to motivate us to rely on our own power, ability, talents, and skills (2 Corinthians 4:4). Satan constantly tries to influence us to think thoughts like: why pray? Do you really need to share your thoughts with God? Doesn't God already know what you are about to say anyway? Is prayer really powerful and effective?

Perhaps I'll say a token, "our Father prayer" and that should be enough for me.

Jesus prayed. He even knew certain situations were going to happen before he prayed, but he still prayed (John 11:14-15; 42). There were certain miracles that the apostles tried to perform by their 'own power,' but Jesus told them, "this kind can only come out by prayer" (Mark 9:29). Jesus lived a life of reliance on the Father. He was intimate with him through prayer, and he asked for situations to be done by prayer. Let us imitate his prayer life.

As we read, ponder and meditate on these passages, let us devote ourselves to nurturing a powerful prayer life – daily! Jesus depended on the Father in all circumstances. He praised, adored, and lavished the Father with love and affection. His dependence on the Father gave him the power to accomplish amazing feats in life. Our prayer life can do the same for us too. The best part of a devoted prayer life is developing a deeper friendship with God! A powerful prayer life is one where we rely on God *all day long*. It is a challenge to put into practice, but if we do, we will have a peace and contentment that passes understanding!

John 17:1-26 (Jesus's longest prayer – An amazing example)

> After Jesus said this, he looked toward heaven and prayed: "Father, the time has come. Glorify your Son, that your Son may glorify you. For you granted him authority over all people that he might give eternal life to all those you have given him. Now this is eternal life: that they may know you, the only true God, and Jesus Christ, whom you have sent. I have brought you glory on earth by completing the work you gave me to do. And now, Father, glorify me in your presence with the glory I had with you before the world began.

"I have revealed you to those whom you gave me out of the world. They were yours; you gave them to me and they have obeyed your word. Now they know that everything you have given me comes from you. For I gave them the words you gave me and they accepted them. They knew with certainty that I came from you, and they believed that you sent me. I pray for them. I am not praying for the world, but for those you have given me, for they are yours. All I have is yours, and all you have is mine. And glory has come to me through them. I will remain in the world no longer, but they are still in the world, and I am coming to you. Holy Father, protect them by the power of your name–the name you gave me–so that they may be one as we are one. While I was with them, I protected them and kept them safe by that name you gave me. None has been lost except the one doomed to destruction so that Scripture would be fulfilled. I am coming to you now, but I say these things while I am still in the world, so that they may have the full measure of my joy within them. I have given them your word and the world has hated them, for they are not of the world any more than I am of the world. My prayer is not that you take them out of the world but that you protect them from the evil one. They are not of the world, even as I am not of it. Sanctify them by the truth; your word is truth. As you sent me into the world, I have sent them into the world. For them I sanctify myself, that they too may be truly sanctified.

"My prayer is not for them alone. I pray also for those who will believe in me through their message, that all of them may be one, Father, just as you are in me and I am in you. May they also be in us so that the world may believe that you have sent me. I have given them the glory that you gave me, that they may be one as we are one: I in them and you in me. May they be brought to complete unity to let the world know that you sent me and have loved them even as you have loved me. "Father, I want those you have given me to be with me where I am, and to see my glory, the glory you have given me because you loved me before the creation of the world. "Righteous Father, though the world does not know you, I know you, and they know that you have sent me. I have made you known to them, and will continue to make you known in order that the love you have for me may be in them and that I myself may be in them."

Mark 1:35: "Very in the morning, while it was still dark, Jesus got up, left the house and went off to a solitary place, where he prayed."

Matthew 5:44: "...and pray for those who persecute you that you may be sons of your Father in heaven."

Matthew 6:6: "But when you pray, go into your room, close the door and *pray to your Father,* who is unseen. *Then your Father,* who sees what is done in secret, will reward you" (Emphasis mine).

Note: Notice how Jesus encourages us with the words *"your Father."* Let's depend on him as child depends on his dad. The Father desires to be close to us. He wants to reward us with more of himself, but we must invest our time walking with him in prayer.

Matthew 14:23: "After he had dismissed them, he went up on a mountainside to pray."

Matthew 21:22: "If you believe, you will receive whatever you ask for in prayer."

Matthew 26:41: "Watch and pray so that you will not fall into temptation."

Mark 11:24: "Therefore I tell you, whatever you ask for in prayer, believe that you received it, and it will be yours. And when you stand praying, if you hold anything against anyone, forgive him, so that your Father in heaven may forgive your sins."

Luke 3:21: "'When all the people were being baptized, Jesus was baptized too. And as he was praying, heaven was opened and the Holy Spirit descended on him in bodily for like a dove. And a voice came from heaven: 'You are my Son, whom I love; with you I am well pleased.'"

Luke 5:16: "But Jesus *often withdrew* to lonely places and prayed" (emphasis mine).

Luke 6:12: "One of those days Jesus went out to a mountainside to pray, and spent the night praying to God."

Luke 6:28: "...pray for those who mistreat you."

Luke 9:18: "'Once when Jesus was praying in private and his disciples were with him, he asked them, 'Who do the crowds say I am?'"

Luke 9:28: "As he was praying, the appearance of his face changed, and his clothes became as bright as a flash of lightening."

Luke 10:21: "'At that time Jesus, full of joy through the Holy Spirit, said, 'I praise you, Father, Lord of heaven and earth, because you have hidden these things from the wise and learned, and revealed them to little children. Yes, Father, for this was your good pleasure.'"

Luke 11:9: "So I say to you: Ask and it will be given to you; seek and you will find; knock and the door will be open to you. For everyone who asks receives; he who seeks finds; and to him knocks the door will be open."

Luke 18:1: "Then Jesus told his disciples a parable to show them that they *should always pray and not give up*" (emphasis mine).

Luke 22:31: "Simon, Simon, Satan has asked to sift you as wheat. But I have prayed for you, Simon, that your faith may not fail. And when you have turned back, strengthen your brothers."

Luke 22:39; 41: "Jesus went out as usual to the Mount of Olives, and his disciples followed him. He withdrew about a stone's throw beyond them, knelt down and prayed."

Luke 22:44: "And being in anguish, he prayed more earnestly, and his sweat was like drops of blood falling to the ground."

John 11:41: "'So they took away the stone. *Then Jesus looked up* and said, 'Father, I thank you that you have heard me. I knew that you always hear me'" (emphasis mine).

John 17:1: "After Jesus said this, *he looked toward heaven* and prayed (emphasis mine).

John 14:13: "And I will do whatever you ask in my name, so that the Son may bring glory to the Father. You may ask me for anything in my name, and I will do it."

John 16:23: "I tell you the truth, my Father will give you whatever you ask in my name."

John 16:24: "Until now you have not asked for anything in my name. Ask and you will receive, and your joy will be complete."

Below are some additional passages from other writers of scripture on prayer. These verses also serve as good reminders that prayer is about building a deeper friendship with God. He will answer some of our requests, and when he does, we should run to him with gratitude and praise! If he doesn't answer a specific prayer, it may not be according to his will or we may be lacking the attitude of the persistent widow (Luke 18:1-8). I hope these passages inspire you to grow in your desire to be with him more.

2 Chronicles 15:2: "The Lord is with you when you are with him."

Acts 16:25: "About midnight Paul and Silas were praying and singing hymns to God, and the other prisoners were listening to them."

Romans 12:12: "Be joyful in hope, patient in affliction, and *faithful in prayer*" (emphasis mine).

Colossians 4:2: "Devote yourselves to prayer..."

1 Thessalonians 5:17: "Pray continually."

Hebrews 4:16: "Let us then approach the throne of grace with confidence, so that we may receive mercy and find grace to help us in our time of need."

James 1:6: "But when he asks, he must believe and not doubt, because he who doubts is like a wave of the sea, blown and tossed by the wind."

James 4:2: "You do not have, because you do not ask God."

James 4:3: "When you ask, you do not receive, because you ask with wrong motives, that you may spend what you get on your pleasures."

James 5:16: "The prayer of a righteous man is powerful and effective."

1 Peter 4:7: "Therefore be clear minded and self-controlled so that you can pray."

1 John 5:14: "This is the confidence we have in approaching God: that if we ask anything according to his will, he hears us."

Psalm 5:3: "In the morning, O Lord, you hear my voice; in the morning I lay my requests before you and wait in expectation."

Psalm 18:6: "In my distress I called to the Lord; I cried to my God for help. From his temple he heard my voice; my cry came before him, into his ears."

Psalm 34:15: "They eyes of the Lord are on the righteous and his ears are attentive to their cry."

Psalm 42:8: "By day the Lord directs his love, at night his song is with me—a prayer to the God of my life."

Psalm 66:18: "If I **cherished sin** in my heart, the Lord would not have listened and heard my voice in prayer" (emphasis mine).

Note: This verse from David's psalm shows us a major hindrance to God's willingness to hear our prayers— unconfessed sin. Some might ask, "If sin prevents God from hearing our prayers, then none of us have a chance, because we all sin, even after we're saved."

A careful reading of this verse however, draws our attention to the word "cherished." "If I had *cherished* sin..." To cherish sin means to embrace it. To love it, hold on to it, and refuse to give it up. This is vastly different from committing a sin that we regret, confess, and forsake as soon as the Holy Spirit brings it to our attention. God doesn't expect us to be sinless, but he does call us to deal with our sin as soon as possible (1 John 1:9). http://www.crosswalk.com/faith/ prayer/10-most-important-verses-on-prayer-in-the-bible.html

Psalm 145:18: "The Lord is near to all who call on him, to all who call on him in truth."

Daniel 9:18: "We do not make requests of you because we are righteous, but because of your great mercy."

ADDITIONAL NOTES

Chapter 17
Several Psalms of Praise

*M*emorizing Psalms can help us grow in our worship of
God. As we put them on our heart, they will become
our heart; enabling us to have a greater connection in our praise
and adoration of Him. This is the kind of worship the Father
seeks. (John 4:23). The following Psalms memorized have helped
me tremendously in my praise of God.

Psalm 19

> The heavens declare the glory of God; the skies
> proclaim the work of his hands. Day after day the
> pour forth speech; night after night they display
> knowledge. There is no speech or language where
> their voice is not heard. Their voice goes out into
> all the earth, their words to the ends of the world.
> In the heavens he has pitched a tent for the sun,
> which is like a bridegroom coming forth from
> his pavilion, like a champion rejoicing to run his
> course. It rises at one of the heavens and makes
> it circuit to the other; nothing is hidden from its
> heat. The law of the Lord is perfect reviving the
> soul. The statutes of the Lord are trustworthy,
> making wise the simple. The precepts of the Lord

are right, giving joy to the heart. The commands of the Lord are radiant, giving light to the eyes. The ordinances of the Lord are sure and altogether righteous. They are more precious than gold, than much pure gold; they are sweeter than honey, than honey from the comb. By them your servant is warned; in keeping them there is great reward. Who can discern his errors? Forgive my hidden faults. Keep your servant also from willful sins; may they not rule over me. Then will I be blameless, innocent of great transgression. May the words of my mouth and the meditation of my heart be pleasing in your sight, O Lord, my Rock and my Redeemer.

Psalm 23

The Lord is my shepherd, I shall not be in want. He makes me lie down in green pastures, he leads me beside quiet waters, he restores my soul. He guides me in paths of righteousness for his name's sake. Even though I walk through the valley of the shadow of death, I will fear no evil, for you are with me; your rod and your staff they comfort me. You prepare a table before me in the presences of my enemies. You anoint my head with oil; my cup overflows. Surely goodness and love will follow me all the days of my life, and I will dwell in the house of the Lord forever.

Psalm 51

Have mercy on me, O God, according to your unfailing love; according to your great compassion blot out my transgressions. Wash away all my iniquity and cleanse me from my sin. For I know my transgressions, and my sin is always before me. Against you, you only, have I sinned and done what is evil in your sight, so that you are proved right when you speak and justified when you judge. Surely I was sinful at birth, sinful from the time my mother conceived me. Surely you desire truth in the inner parts; you teach me wisdom in the inmost place. Cleanse me with hyssop, and I will be clean; wash me, and I will be whiter than snow. Let me hear joy and gladness; let the bones you have crushed rejoice. Hide your face from my sins and blot out all my iniquity. Create in me a pure heart, O God, and renew a steadfast spirit within me. Do not cast me from your presence or take your Holy Spirit from me. Restore to me the joy of your salvation and grant me a willing spirit, to sustain me. Then I will teach transgressors your ways, and sinners will turn back to you. Save me from bloodguilt, O God, the God who saves me, and my tongue will sing of your righteousness. O Lord, open my lips, and my mouth will declare your praise. You do not delight in sacrifice, or I would bring it; you do not take pleasure in burnt offerings. The sacrifices of God are a broken spirit; a broken and contrite heart, O God, you will not despise. In your good pleasure make Zion prosper; build up the walls of Jerusalem. Then there will be righteous sacrifices, whole burnt offerings to delight you; then bulls will be offered on your altar.

Psalm 63

O God, you are my God, earnestly I seek you; my soul thirsts for you, my body longs for you, in a dry and weary land where there is no water. I have seen you in the sanctuary and beheld your power and your glory. Because your love is better than life, my lips will glorify you. I will praise you as long as I live, and in your name I will lift up my hands. My soul will be satisfied as with the richest of foods; with singing lips my mouth will praise you. On my bed I remember you; I think of you through the watches of the night, because you are my help, I sing in the shadow of your wings. My soul clings to you; your right hand upholds me. They who seek my life will be destroyed; they will go down to the depths of the earth. They will be given over to the sword and become food for jackals. But the king will rejoice in God; all who swear by God's name will praise him, while the mouths of liars will be silenced.

Psalm 93

The Lord reigns, he is robed in majesty; the Lord is robed in majesty and is armed with strength. The world is firmly established; it cannot be moved. Your throne was established long ago; you are from all eternity. The seas have lifted up, O Lord, the seas have lifted up their voice; the seas have lifted up their pounding waves. Mightier than the thunder of the great waters, mightier than the breakers of the sea—the Lord on high is mighty. Your statutes stand firm; holiness adorns your house for endless days, O Lord.

Psalm 100

Shout for joy to the Lord, all the earth. Worship the Lord with gladness; come before him with joyful songs. Know that the Lord is God. It is he who made us, and we are his; we are his people, the sheep of his pasture. Enter his gates with thanksgiving and his courts with praise; give thanks to him and praise his name. For the Lord is good and his love endures forever; his faithfulness continues through all generations.

Psalm 139

O Lord, you have searched me and you know me. You know when I sit and when I rise; you perceive my thoughts from afar. You discern my going out and my lying down; you are familiar with all my ways. Before a word is on my tongue you know it completely, O Lord. You hem me in—behind and before; you have laid your hand upon me. such knowledge is too wonderful for me, too lofty for me to attain. Where can I go from your Spirit? Where can I flee from your presence? If I go up to the heavens, you are there; if I make my bed in the depths, you are there. If I rise on the wings of the dawn, if I settle on the far side of the sea, even there your hand will guide me, your right hand will hold me fast. If I say, "Surely the darkness will hide me and the light become night around me," even the darkness will not be dark to you;

the night will shine like the day, for darkness is as light to you. For you created my inmost being; you knit me together in my mother's womb. I praise you because I am fearfully and wonderfully made; your works are wonderful, I know that full well. My frame was not hidden from you when I was made in the secret place. When I was woven together in the depths of the earth, your eyes saw my unformed body. All the days ordained for me were written in your book before one of them came to be. How precious to me are your thoughts, O God! How vast is the sum of them! Were I to count them, they would outnumber the grains of sand. When I awake, I am still with you. If only you would slay the wicked, O God! Away from me, you bloodthirsty men! They speak of you with evil intent; your adversaries misuse your name. Do I not hate those who hate you, O Lord, and abhor those who rise up against you? I have nothing but hatred for them; I count them my enemies. Search me, O God, and know my heart; test me and know my anxious thoughts. See if there is any offensive way in me, and lead me in the way of everlasting.

Psalm 145

I will exalt you, my God the King; I will praise your name for ever and ever. Every day I will praise you and extol your name for ever and ever. Great is the Lord and most worthy of praise; his greatness no one can fathom. One generation will commend your works to another; they will tell of your mighty acts. They will speak of the glorious splendor of your majesty, and I will meditate on your wonderful works. They will tell of the power of your awesome works, and I will proclaim your great deeds. They will celebrate your abundant goodness and joyfully sing of your righteousness. The Lord is gracious and compassionate, slow to anger and rich in love. The Lord is good to all; he has compassion on all he has made. All you have made will praise you, O Lord; your saints will extol you. They will tell of the glory of your kingdom and speak of your might, so that all men may know of your mighty acts and the glorious splendor of your kingdom. Your kingdom is an everlasting kingdom, and your dominion endures through all generations. The Lord is faithful to all his promises and loving toward all he has made. The Lord upholds all those who fall and lifts up all who are bowed down. The eyes of all look to you, and you give them their food at the proper time. You open your hand and satisfy the desires of every living thing. The Lord is righteous in all his ways and loving toward all he has made. The Lord is near to all who call on him, to all who call on him in truth. He fulfills the desires of those who fear him; he hears their cry and saves them. The Lord watches over all who love him, but all the wicked he will destroy. My mouth will speak in praise of the Lord. Let every creature praise his holy name for ever and ever.

Psalm 148

Praise the Lord. Praise the Lord from the heavens, praise him in the heights above. Praise him, all his angels, praise him, all his heavenly hosts. Praise him, sun and moon, praise him, all you shining stars. Praise him, you highest heavens and you waters above the skies. Let them praise the name of the Lord, for he commanded and they were created. He set them in place for ever and ever; he gave a decree that will never pass away. Praise the Lord from the earth, you great sea creatures and all ocean depths, lightning and hail, snow and clouds, stormy winds that do his bidding, you mountains and all hills, fruit trees and all cedars, wild animals and all cattle, small creatures and flying birds, kings of the earth and all nations, you princes and all rulers on earth, young men and maidens, old men and children. Let them praise the name of the Lord, for his name alone is exalted; his splendor is above the earth and the heavens. He has raised up for his people a horn, the praise of all his saints, of Israel, the people close to his heart. Praise the Lord.

ADDITIONAL NOTES

Chapter 18
Fun Brain Facts

15 Amazing Facts: (ebook 70 amazing facts about your brain by Tim Brownson)

1. You have a finite amount of will power each day because to exercise will power you need energy in the form of oxygen and glucose. That is why it's harder to say "no" when you are tired or not feeling yourself.

2. A thought is a physical pathway in the brain. The more you have that thought the more you groove that path and the easier it is to have it again. That's why having the thought *"Why do I suck?"* is never a great idea.

3. Reading out loud to kids accelerates their brain development.

4. Reframing negative events in a positive light literally rewires your brain and can make you a happier person, as can regular meditation.

5. The brain is approximately 75% water, but you should never drink it.

6. Your brain only weighs about 3lbs yet the greedy thing uses between 20% and 25% of your energy supplies each day.

7. There are approximately 10 to the power of 60 atoms in the universe. Your brain laughs in the face of that figure

however, as it has 10 to the power of 1,000,000 different ways it can wire itself up. That's the number 10 followed up with 1 million zeroes, which is to all intents and purposes an infinite amount of ways.

8. Speaking of large numbers, there are approximately 1.1 trillion cells and 100 billion neurons in the average human brain.

9. The slowest speed information passes around your brain is approximately 260 mph

10. If you lose blood flow to your brain you will last about 10 second before you pass out.

11. Leaving aside degenerative brain disease, your brain never loses the ability to learn and change because it's effectively plastic and constantly rewiring itself. Leopards may indeed not change their spots, but you're not a Leopard and you can change yourself and your brain is up for the challenge.

12. It's a myth that we only use 10 percent of our brains; we use it all. If you don't believe me, cut a bit out and see what happens.

13. Until relatively recently scientists thought that the brain was the only area of the human body that didn't generate new cells. We now know that's not true and the brain does reproduce shiny new cells for you to use.

14. You have something in your brain called mirror neurons. If you see somebody stub their toe for example, the same pain area will light up in your own brain causing you to flinch. Mirror neurons weren't even known to exist prior to the early 1990's, but now there is a growing belief in the scientific community they are responsible for us feeling empathy toward others.

15. The brain is very poor at concentrating for long periods of time and needs to clear it's head so to speak about every 90 minutes or so. You should take lots of mini breaks rather than one long break for lunch.

12 Surprising Memory Facts by The CEU Group by Justin Barton
(http://www.theceugroup.com/12-surprising-human-memory-facts)

Do you remember what you ate for breakfast this morning? If the image of a plate of eggs and bacon popped into your mind, that memory was the result of an incredibly complex power— one that reassembled various memory impressions from a web- like patter of cells scattered throughout our brain. Daily, our brain processes information while all of the different systems work together perfectly to provide a cohesive thought. Thanks to memory, we are able to store, preserve and reproduce information.

Here are twelve interesting facts about the human memory— if you can remember them!

1. Scientific research has shown that the human brain starts remembering things from the womb—memory begins to work twenty weeks after conception.
2. Memory has two components—short term and long term. Most short-term memories only last to seconds.
3. Memory is influenced by a variety of factors. Memory based on what you saw vs what you hear is called visual and auditory memory.
4. The storage capacity of the human brain is virtually limitless.
5. Caffeine doesn't maintain memory performances, it only increases alertness.
6. It is believed that an adult can remember twenty to one hundred thousand words.
7. Sleep is important to memory. Although scientists don't know exactly how it affects the brain, it has been shown that sleep aids storage and retrieval of long-term memories.
8. Many people associate memory loss with aging. However, the memory loss we see the older we get is generally because we tend to exercise our brains less as we age.

9. Your memory can associate a scent with a certain event or occurrence. A smell can trigger the memory in your mind associated with it. The hippocampus is the part of the brain largely responsible for the formation of new memories and directly interacts with our sense of smell.

10. There is such a thing as "false memory." Researchers are beginning to understand that the human mind can create, exaggerate, distort, or re-invent a memory after a traumatic experience or something that impacted them greatly.

11. The mind must be exercised just like any other muscle in the body. The harder you think about a memory, the more likely you are to remember it accurately. Thinking will create a stronger link between active neurons.

12. We are more likely to remember the information that is provided if it is in a weird, difficult-to-read font.

How to Remember 90% of Everything You Learn by Sean Kim
http://www.lifehack.org/399140/how-to-remember-90-of-everything-you-learn
How humans remember:

5% of what they learn when they've learned from a lecture (i.e., lectures)

10% of what they learn when they've learned from reading (i.e., books, articles)

20% of what they learn from audio-visual (i.e., videos)

30% of what they learn when they see a demonstration

50% of what they learn when engaged in a group discussion.

75% of what they learn when they practice what they learned.

90% of what they learn when they use it immediately (teach others)

Afterword
Letter to My children

To Ethan, Elliot, and Brinkley,

Your mom and I are thankful to God for each of you. You are gifts of love. We can't imagine what life would be like without you. Each of you has positively impacted our hearts over the years. On the one hand, we are excited to see how God will move in your lives as you carve out a life independent of us. On the other hand, we will be sad not to have you around on a regular basis. We enjoy being with you that much!

I wrote this book with each of you in mind. Ethan, Elliot, and Brinkley, you are special to us. In the first part of the book, I share a few thoughts about how memorizing Scripture has impacted my life. The second half of the book are topics for you to study when you're ready. It is my deepest hope they motivate you to become a lifelong student and doer of God's Word. We're not sure how many years God has left for Mom and me. However, before we leave this world, we want you to know what's of supreme importance to us: nothing is more important than developing an intimate walk with God. Nothing.

We have so much fun talking with you about your dreams for the future. We look forward to hearing about your adventures, where you've traveled, what hobbies you're developing, the music you're into, the career path you're on, the friendships you're forming, and so much more. And I'm sure we will continue to talk about your dreams and aspirations with each passing year.

However, I humbly believe that without God at the center of your life, everything is a chasing after the wind. Of course, you know how futile it is to chase wind. You'll never catch it. Similarly, if you choose to make anything this world offers as the centerpiece of your life, it is like trying to capture wind. You'll be dissatisfied, frustrated, and empty. God is the only one who can fill you to the full.

This book is the legacy we leave for you to know what our one holy passion is: to love God with all our heart, mind, soul, and strength.

Each of you have a unique life journey to travel. Be the best you that you can be. Don't try to be someone else. Don't compare yourself with others, for you'll never measure up. Be you. There is only one of you in the entire universe. Nurture and develop your talents and abilities. We have no idea where your steps will take you or where your paths will lead. We pray that one day you will decide to make Jesus your best friend and Lord of your lives. No one else is more important for you to get to know. No matter where life may take you, no matter how good or difficult life may be, the only thing that counts when your race of life is finished, is entering heaven.

The Christian life is not an easy journey. Actually, it is, perhaps, the most challenging decision we've ever made. But it sure has been rewarding! Nothing compares to knowing Jesus. Offer us all the money, fame, and wealth the world has to offer in place of Jesus, and we'd say, "No thanks. He's all we need."

We hope one day you'll say the same. We love you with an undying love.

Dad and Mom
September 1, 2017

Acknowledgments

Thank you, Boston Campus Ministry, for inspiring me to be my best for God as a college student (1987–1992). If not for my brother Mike introducing me to Jesus and his church, the special memories created throughout these years would never have happened. Mike has been a dear brother and faithful friend to me and many others in God's kingdom over the years. Thank you.

Although my dad and mom are not alive, I'm thankful for the unconditional love they showered on my brother and me. I wouldn't be the man I am today if not for their support and influence on my life. Sadly, my mom passed away in 2016, but happily, she was a disciple of Jesus.

Tommy Alessi, you were one of a kind, a friend who stuck closer than a brother. I miss your stories and laughter. I can't wait to see you again.

Steve Rosenbaum, thanks for your unwavering love and vision for me over the years. You have been a great encourager to me and my family. I'm thankful to count you as a friend. Thanks for loving us.

The gang of friends from Massachusetts whom I'll always cherish, respect, honor, and appreciate: Kevin McDaniel, Chip Mitchell, Dan Moroney, Steve Miller, Bruce Miller, Jason Gangelhoff, Charles Middelhof, Jeff Chartrand, Tom Heaton, Jim Bolton, Andrew Beaudry, Paul Sheridan, Deon Candia, Sam Iturino, Bob Aho, Mike Sawyer, Kip Harms, ***and many others***.

You taught me not to take life so seriously and that openness breeds openness. You showed me the value of true friendship. You were the iron that sharpened me to be my best for God. Thanks for being my friends through thick and thin. Thanks for teaching me to enjoy life as I walk with God. You're eternally etched on my heart.

Thanks for all the great memories, Pioneer Valley Church. You will always hold a special place in my heart.

Though I was in a spiritual wasteland during my years in Charlotte, North Carolina, I thank Ron and Lavonia Drabot for the unconditional love they showered on me and my family.

Chris Davis (aka, Crazy Horse), thanks for being a good friend and a "Barnabas" to me over the years.

Thank you, Savannah church, especially the group in Bluffton/Hilton Head, for loving me and my family. We look forward to building greater friendships that last a life-time.

Thank you, old-time preachers for your inspiration, sacrifice, and labor of love in the Lord over the years. I still listen to your sermons on cassette tapes—it was that long ago. You changed my life through your words! You know who you are. There are too many to list by name.

Nina Ibarra, you have a heart of gold. Thank you for being a friend and helping with the early edits! Thanks for giving me the nudge I needed.

Thank you, Erin Brown with 'The Write Editor'! You have a way with words. Thanks for stepping in at the eleventh hour to help refine this manuscript even further.

Notes

Introduction

1. Linda Melone and Sarah McNaughton, "10 Brain Exercises that Boost Brain Memory," *Everyday Health*, April 2016, http://www.everydayhealth.com/longevity/mental-fitness/brain-exercises-for-memory.aspx.
2. Melinda Smith and Lawrence Robinson, "How to Improve your Memory," Helpguide.org, https://www.helpguide.org/articles/healthy-living/how-to-improve-your-memory.htm.

Chapter 1

1. Matthew Hart, *Gold: The Race for the Most Seductive Metal* (NY: Simon & Schuster, 2013), 1–8.
2. Josh McDowell, *The New Evidence that Demands a Verdict* (Campus Crusade for Christ, 1999), 4.
3. Ibid., 3–8.
4. Margaret Daly-Denton, *Brad Sherrill's Performance, Scripture in Church Magazine,* July-September 2008, #151.

Chapter 2

1. Jay Karlson, "Top 10 Most Dangerous Countries for Christians," November 2011, *Listverse*, http://listverse.com/2011/11/24/top-10-most-dangerous-countries-for-christians/.

Chapter 3

1. William Manchester and Paul Reid, The Last Lion: William Spencer Churchill: Defender of the Realm, 1940–1965 (NY: Little, Brown and Company, 2012), 1032.
2. As told by David Stanley, *Did Elvis Commit Suicide? Life Magazine*, June 1990, 101.
3. Bill Hybels, *Too Busy Not to Pray: Slowing Down to Be with God* (Downers Grove, IL: Inter-Varsity Press, 1988), 66.

Chapter 4

1. Gerald Coffee, *Beyond Survival* (NY: Coffee Enterprises, 1990).
2. Deepak Chopra, "Why Meditate?" *Deepak Chopra* (blog), www.deepakchopra.com/blog/article/4701.

Chapter 5

1. McDowell, *The New Evidence that Demands a Verdict*, 10.
2. Bart Baggett, *Success Secrets of the Rich & Happy* (LA: Empressé Publishing, 2001), 90.
3. Vivian Giang, "What It Takes to Change Your Brain's Pattern after Age 25," *Fast Company*, April 2015, https://www.fastcompany.com/3045424
4. Eric Gardner, "Learn about the Power and Potential of Your Brain," *Bookboon* (blog), http://bookboon.com/blog/2013/10/learn-about-the-power-and-potential-of-your-brain/.

Chapter 8

1. John Foxe, *Foxe's Book of Martyrs*, Blacksburg, VA, Wilder Publications 2009, 9.

Chapter 11

1. Dr. Ray Pritchard, "How Many Times Shall I Forgive My Brother?" *Christianity Today*, http://www.christianity.com/dr-ray-pritchard/how-many-times-shall-i-forgive-my-brother.html.

Chapter 12

1. Doug Greenwold, "Being a First-Century Disciple," February 2007, https://bible.org/article/being-first-century-disciple.